ON

NIETZSCHE

Eric Steinhart
William Paterson University

Wadsworth
Thomson Learning

Australia • Canada • Denmark • Japan • Mexico • New Zealand • Philippines
Puerto Rico • Singapore • Spain • United Kingdom • United States

Printed in the United States of America
4 5 6 7 03 02

For permission to use material from this text, contact us:
Web: www.thomsonrights.com
Fax: 1-800-730-2215
Phone: 1-800-730-2214

For more information, contact:
Wadsworth/Thomson Learning
10 Davis Drive
Belmont, CA 94002-3098
USA
www.wadsworth.com

ISBN: 0-534-57606-0

On Nietzsche

Nietzsche's Books

Nietzsche's books are usually cited by giving an abbreviation for the book followed by a section number. For example: GS 341 is *section 341* of *The Gay Science*. Section numbers are *not* page numbers. In some books, Nietzsche groups the sections into divisions. So, GM 3:4 is section 4 of division 3 of *The Genealogy of Morals*. The numbering is the same in all editions. All these books are inexpensive and easy to get. I indicate how each book is cited and the translation I use.

UM   *Untimely Meditations*. Cited by division and page. Trans. R. J. Hollingdale (New York: Cambridge University Press, 1983).

PTG   *Philosophy in the Tragic Age of the Greeks*. Cited by section. Trans. M. Cowan (Washington: Regnery Publishing 1996).

HH I   *Human All Too Human*. Volume 1. Cited by section. Trans. R. J. Hollingdale. (New York: Cambridge University. Press, 1986).

AOM   *Assorted Opinions and Maxims*. Part 1 of Volume 2 of *Human All Too Human*. Cited by section.

WS   *The Wanderer and His Shadow* Part 2 of Volume 2 of *Human All Too Human*. Cited by section.

D   *Daybreak*. Cited by section. Trans. R. J. Hollingdale (New York: Cambridge University Press, 1982).

GS   *The Gay Science*. Cited by section. Trans. W. Kaufmann (New York: Random House, 1974).

Z   *Thus Spake Zarathustra*. Cited by division and section. Trans. R. J. Hollingdale (New York: Penguin Books, 1969).

BGE   *Beyond Good and Evil*. Cited by section. Trans. W. Kaufmann (New York: Random House, 1966).

GM   *The Genealogy of Morals*. Cited by division and section. Trans. F. Golffing (New York: Doubleday, 1956).

TI   *Twilight of the Idols.* Cited by division and section. Trans. R. J. Hollingdale. (New York: Penguin Books, 1984).

AC   *The Antichrist.* Cited by section. Trans. R. J. Hollingdale. (New York: Penguin Books, 1984).

EH   *Ecce Homo.* Cited by division and section. Trans. R. J. Hollingdale. (New York: Penguin Books, 1983).

PT   *Philosophy and Truth.* Cited by section and page number. Trans. D. Breazeale (London: Humanities Press, 1979).

WP   *The Will to Power.* Cited by section. Trans. W. Kaufmann & R. J. Hollingdale (New York: Random House, 1968).

1

Introduction

1. Mind as the Mirror of World

While many traditional philosophers and religious authorities say that our minds are not parts of this world, Nietzsche says our minds are parts of the world. He says they reflect the world from the inside:

> man has evolved slowly, and knowledge is still evolving: his picture of the world thus becomes ever more true and complete. Naturally it is only a clearer and clearer *mirroring*. But the mirror itself is nothing entirely foreign and apart from the nature of things. On the contrary, it too slowly arose as [part of] the nature of things. We observe an effort to make the mirror more and more adequate. The natural process is carried on by science. Thus the things mirror themselves ever more clearly (PT p. 37-38; see HH I:2, I:10, I:16; GS 354; BGE 207, 295)

In human consciousness, a part of the world is naturally aware of the whole world. The human mind is the eye with which the world looks at itself. It is the self-mirroring, the self-reflection, of the world. But since our minds are in the world, they are eyes that sees themselves. We are self-aware. In human self-consciousness, the mirror reflects itself. But when a mirror reflects itself, it reflects its own reflection: it reflects itself reflecting itself forever, making a series of endlessly nested self-reflections. If you point a television camera at the very television screen on which its output is displayed, you get a feedback loop: the TV shows an endless series of TV screens inside TV screens. Our minds are like cameras pointed partly at the world, partly at their own self-conscious self-display.

1

2. Mind as the Mirror of Mind

The endlessly self-nested series of reflections within reflections is what Nietzsche calls *the inner world* (WP 476-480). The inner world is a labyrinth of strangely distorted self-reflections.[1] If you connect a microphone to an amplifier, and connect the amplifier to a speaker, and then put the microphone in front of the speaker, any background noise is amplified by the feedback until it becomes a distorted howl. If a TV screen amplifies the light absorbed by its camera, and if that camera points at the screen so that the amplified light gets projected back into the camera, then with each cycle through the feedback loop the light is brighter and more focused. Each self-reflection of the TV screen displays a brighter TV screen. The series of self-reflections of screens in screens ends in a single solar point, bright as the sun. The self-reflection of the mind is a feedback loop just like that: the mind magnifies its own light and feeds it back into itself. The inner world is full of fires and shadows, "phantoms and false lights" (TI 6:3).

According to Nietzsche, the bright focal point of the mind's own self-magnified light is God. God is a reflection that the mind mistakes for something else. God is a shining impostor that makes man look small and dark. If man compares himself with God, "it is because he looks into this brilliant mirror that his own nature seems to him so dismal, so uncommonly distorted" (HH I:132); but Nietzsche says we must recognize that this mirroring is a mental error, so "that the man in this condition has gotten into it, not through his 'guilt' and 'sin', but through a succession of errors of reason, that it was the fault of the mirror if his nature appeared to him dark and hateful to such a degree, and that this mirror was his work" (HH I:133).

Mirrors are surfaces, but surfaces cover depths. Each reflection in the series of endlessly self-nested mirrorings is deeper than the last. The series of reflections in reflections is like a series of steps leading down into the deep underworld of the mind. Caves are labyrinths. Plato said that the world in which we live, move, and have our being is like a cave in which we are prisoners, and that all our experience is only shadows cast on cave-walls. For Nietzsche, the subterranean inner world is a cave haunted by vampires and ghosts. It is haunted by superstitious fears: fear of death, of ghosts, of Hell, and of God.

God is the brightest light in the inner world. God is an underground sun. But the brightest light casts the darkest shadows. Nietzsche is famous for his slogan "God is dead" (GS 125, 343). But God is dead like a *vampire* who feeds on the blood of the living (GS 372). God is dead, but "there may still be caves for thousands of years in which his shadow will be shown" (GS 108). These shadows of God darken our minds (GS 109). Yet they are only the ghostly shadows cast by our own fearful self-delusions. We are haunted by our own distorted self-images: "Do you not fear to re-encounter in the cave of every kind of knowledge your own ghost -- the ghost which is the veil behind which truth has hidden itself from you?" (D 539).

3. Looking at the World from the Inside

The mind reflects itself because it is a part of the world that looks at the whole world from the inside. So, it sees itself seeing the whole world, which implies that it sees itself seeing itself seeing the whole world, and so on. The mind reflects the world by making a map of the world in its thoughts; it makes a conceptual map of the world.

Maps are like mirror images. A map reflects the territory of which it is a map. If a map of Vermont is spread out on a table in a room in a house in Vermont, that map is like a mirror of Vermont that reflects Vermont from the inside. Any map of Vermont from inside Vermont is an internal self-representation of Vermont. Likewise, every map of the world from the inside is an *internal self-representation* of the world. It is a map of the world from an internal standpoint, from an internal point of view. Every human mind contains such a map. Our maps of the world are symbolic. They are conceptual schemes.[2]

A conceptual map of the whole world from inside the world is what Nietzsche calls an *interpretation* of the world; the relation of the map to the world is what he calls a *perspective*. Since any interpretation of the world is a perspective on it, the two terms mean pretty much the same. An interpretation is a total "world-view"; it is a theory of everything. Since every interpretation of the world is a reflection of the whole world by a part of the world, it is a *self-interpretation*. It is a self-representation of the world. Our minds are like canvases on which the world naturally paints its own self-portraits.

Nietzsche argues that there are no interpretations or maps of the world from the outside. There are no external perspectives on the world. Nietzsche's *perspectivism* is the theory that the human mind strives for realistic internal conceptual maps of the world. It is an example of what Putnam, the 20th Century American thinker, calls *internal realism*.[3] Nietzsche and Putnam both deny that there is any external point of view from which to map the world. The external point of view is usually called the *God's-Eye View*, since God is often thought of as being somehow outside of the world. Nietzsche, like Putnam, denies that there is any God's-Eye View of the world.

4. The World: Space, Time, and Possibility

The reason there are no external perspectives on the world is that there is nothing outside of the world (TI 6:8; WP 765, 1067). Nietzsche's own perspective on the world is from the inside: "And do you know what 'the world' is to me? Shall I show it to you in my mirror?" (WP 1067). The world is far more than the planet Earth, far more than even our entire physical universe. The world extends out both physically and logically from the present situation of your body. It extends out from where you are, when you are, and how you are -- in every spatial, temporal, and logical direction.

To see how the world extends out in every direction, think of our theories of space, time, and possibility. Our theories are conceptual pictures of the extension of reality in space, time, and possibility. At the center of the picture is the present. The *present* is here, now, and actual. *Spatial maps* of the physical universe expand outward from here (where your body is) to cover our Earth, through our solar system, our galaxy, and outward in every spatial direction through ever larger structures, like our local cluster of galaxies.

Timelines are *temporal maps* that depict the history of our physical universe, extending from the now of the present both back into the past and ahead into the future. For example, we have a theoretical picture of the past history of the Earth that extends back to the age of the dinosaurs, and we have a picture of the history of the universe that extends back to its physical origin in the Big Bang. We also have a theoretical picture of the future history of the Earth and universe that extends ahead to the explosion of the sun in a supernova, to the eventually cooling of our physical universe as the stars burn out.

Spatial and temporal maps are familiar enough. Less familiar is the notion of a *possibility map*.[4] The present is the way things actually are. But that is not the only possibility. There are other ways the whole physical universe could be, even though it is not actually that way. Every other possible way for the whole physical universe to be is an other possible physical universe. Other possible universes are more or less logically close to ours depending on how similar they are to the actual universe. For instance, suppose you flip a coin. It possibly comes up either heads or tails, but it actually comes up only one way. If it comes up heads, then there is a possible universe that is exactly like ours except for one difference: the coin comes up tails. A possible universe that differs from the actual one in just one way is just one step away from ours on the possibility map. Universes that differ in many ways are many steps away. All these "alternate" universes are in the world like islands in one ocean.

4

There is no other world besides this world. No matter how far you travel in space, in time, or in possibility, you will never escape from the world.[5] Since the world is closed physically (that is, spatially and temporally), there is no way for the body to get out of the world in order to perceive it from the outside. Since the world is closed logically, there is no way for the mind to get out of the world to think of it from the outside. Any perspective on the world from outside is impossible because it is self-refuting.

5. Self-Reflection and Self-Destruction

Some statements are self-refuting. For instance: "Every rule has an exception". Since "Every rule has an exception" is a rule, it applies to itself. So, it has an exception, which is an exceptionless rule. So, if it is true that "Every rule has an exception", then there is a rule with no exception; but then it is not true that *every* rule has an exception. If you think "Everything I think is false", then your thought applies to itself; it renders itself false. It's a negative self-reflection.

Suppose a person looks into a mirror and says: "Everything reflected in this mirror does not exist". Suppose that what the person says is *true*. Since the person who is looking into the mirror is reflected in the mirror, the person who makes the statement does not exist if the statement is true. But people who do not exist don't talk. They don't make true statements. The person's statement is absurd, because if it is true, then the reflective power of the mirror negates it.

Suppose that the mirror reflects everything in the world, and that a person looks into the mirror and says "Everything reflected in the mirror does not exist". If the statement is true, then everything in the world does not exist. Since the person making the statement is in the world, that person does not exist. Since the mirror is also in the world, the mirror does not exist. But people that do not exist do not make statements, and mirrors that do not exist do not reflect people who do not exist. What the person says cannot be true.

Nietzsche often turns philosophical theories back on themselves, to see if their self-reflections are self-affirming or self-negating, that is, to see if they are consistent or contradictory when they are applied to themselves. Some 19th century thinkers argued that the "external world" we perceive is a product of our bodily organs (such as our brains). To which Nietzsche replies: "But then our body, as a part of this external world, would be the work of our organs! But then our organs themselves would be -- the work of our organs!" (BGE 15). He thinks this is absurd, a self-refuting vicious circle. Nietzsche believes his theories, applied to themselves, are self-consistent (BGE 22).

Suppose that some human mind thinks: "Everything of which I am conscious does not exist". Since this thought is about the mind itself, if it is true, then it applies to itself; but then the mind that thinks it does not exist. Since a mind that does not exist does not think, what that mind thinks is false. The situation is absurd. But if that mind is stubborn, it might *insist* that what it thinks is true. If it insists, then it is in a state of self-deception or self-delusion. So long as that self-deception is merely a thought, it's harmless enough. But thoughts lead to action. Action based on self-delusion is self-destructive.

6. The Self-Delusion of Western Thought

Nietzsche thinks that Western civilization has been in a state of self-delusion for over 2000 years. He argues that Western culture insists on the truth of a negative interpretation of the world, one that denies the reality of the world, that says the world is an illusion, a mirage, or a nightmare. But if it insists that its negative interpretation of the world is true, then its interpretation applies to itself. So, Nietzsche argues, the very mind that denies the reality of the world denies its own reality. Its theory that the world is unreal is self-undermining. It discredits itself. It is self-refuting. To affirm such a self-negating theory is to negate the very self that affirms it. Insofar as the mind follows the logic of that self-negation in its actions, the result is the very real self-destruction of that mind by way of destruction of the entire world. It is suicide by means of world-annihilation.

Nietzsche argues that Western philosophers and religious authorities have traditionally endorsed negative perspective on the world by asserting that there is some *other world* beyond or above this world, a world that is better than this world.[6] The other world is an immaterial spirit world. Nietzsche argues, in particular, that Platonic philosophers and Christian religious authorities have worked hard to negate this world by taking its features and proclaiming that there is some other world with *opposite* features (WP 579).

Supernaturalism says that the other world is a place outside of this world, that it is possible to (conceptually) view this world from the other world, and that the theory of this world as seen from that external perspective (that "God's-Eye View") is the one true theory of this world -- it is the one way this world really is. This world is false; the other world is true. This world is an illusory appearance, full of contradiction; the other world is pure coherent reality. In this world, change makes everything uncertain; the other world is changeless.

Ascetic supernaturalism adds a negative value judgment: seen from this external perspective this world is ugly and evil: "why a Beyond if not as a means of befouling the Here-and-Now?" (TI 9:34); "Reality has been deprived of its value, its meaning, its veracity to the same degree as an ideal world has been fabricated" (EH Foreward 2). So, it is better to be in this supernatural place outside of the world. The other world is our original home (TI 3:5; WP 765); our souls have fallen from there to here, and must return.

Nietzsche worries that ascetic supernaturalism has truly destructive consequences: "The Christian resolve to find the world ugly and bad has made the world ugly and bad" (GS 130). He thinks Christianity works hard to "invert all love of the earthly . . . into hatred of the earth and the earthly" (BGE 62). Ascetic supernaturalism confronts future generations with a terrible choice: "Either abolish your reverences or -- *yourselves!"* (GS 346; cf. GS 343).

7. Self-Delusion and Self-Degradation

Ascetic morality opposes the world. But ascetic morality is part of the world. It is like the mirror that denies its own mirroring: "From the standpoint of morality, the world is false. But to the extent that morality itself is a part of this world, morality is false." (WP 552)

Nietzsche often refers to ascetic supernaturalism using terms like *nihilism* and *pessimism.* If pessimism is true, so that life has no real value, then the self-consistent pessimist is also self-destructive: at the moment of realizing the truth of pessimism, the self-consistent pessimist commits suicide. To believe that pessimism is true, and to stay alive in order to declare verbally or intellectually that life has no value is to be inconsistent. Pessimism is a self-refuting doctrine, in the sense that if it is true then it is not possible for anyone who affirms it to consistently exist: "Pessimism, pure, raw, proves itself only by the self-negation of the pessimists" (TI 9:36). Nietzsche does not worry much about world-suicide. He worries more that nihilism leads to a deep *sickness* -- a self-degradation of life (GM 1, 3). It is a kind of comprehensive anorexia or self-starvation.

If Nietzsche is right that every perspective on the world is internal, so that every perspective on the world takes a perspective on itself, then any negative perspective on the world is negates itself. It is as absurd as the rule that says "Every rule has an exception". Since we are wholly in the world, if we deny the value of the world, we deny the value of our own denial. If we condemn the world, we condemn our condemnation (WP 293; HH I:29). Nihilism undermines itself.

8. From Self-Negation to Objectivity

In ascetic supernaturalism, human minds inside the world condemn the world. If such minds are parts of the world, they condemn their own condemnation; their nihilism refutes itself. The only way to condemn the world consistently is to claim to condemn it from a God's-Eye View, from the outside. One of the most powerful tactics of ascetic supernaturalism is to say that its world-hatred is divine revelation, that nihilism (e.g. Christianity) is God's Absolute Truth. Nietzsche counters that there is no Absolute Truth (WP 540). Some sentences have more than one interpretation. For instance, "Ronald loves jelly beans more than Nancy" has two interpretations: either it means that Ronald loves jelly beans more than Nancy loves jelly beans, or it means that Ronald loves jelly beans more than he loves Nancy. Without further information, there is no way to decide which interpretation is correct. Given only the sentence as evidence, both interpretations are equally valid. Nietzsche thinks the world is like an ambiguous book, that it is text with multiple interpretations (GS 373). Given the world as evidence, its different interpretations are all equally valid. Existence is ambiguous; there are infinitely many equally true perspectives (GS 124, 374; WP 481).

Nietzsche denies that there is any objectively true theory of the world; consequently, he denies that there are any subjectively true theories of the world. Nietzsche refutes subjectivism by turning it back against itself: "'Everything is subjective,' you say; but even this is interpretation" (WP 481). But to deny that there is any objective interpretation is not to deny *objectivity;* he defines objectivity as the coordination of all perspectives (GM 3:12; WP 556). The theory that truth is multiple is perfectly reasonable. It corresponds more closely to the serious facts of logic than the theory that truth is singular.

Nietzsche thinks there are many equally scientific and equally valid ways to interpret empirical facts (that is, the natural phenomena we experience with our senses and instruments). For instance, two physicists may agree that natural processes are calculable (so that math is useful in science), but they may agree about this for very different reasons. The one may say that natural processes are calculable because natural things are ultimately interchangeable atoms whose behaviors are determined by general principles (laws) whose consequences are the empirical facts; the other may say that those processes are calculable because natural things are ultimately all so unique that the only ways they are able to all fit together are ways whose consequences are the empirical facts. These are two different very explanations for the same facts; they are two different interpretations (BGE 22; BGE 15).

In physics there are many versions of quantum mechanics.[7] Each attributes a different structure to our physical universe. Yet given the same data as input, they all produce the same predictions as output. Since they are all equally good at explaining what they are supposed to explain, they are all equally scientifically true. Nietzsche says that the world has no interest in favoring one interpretation over the others, since it is ultimately indifferent (BGE 9). In mathematics, there are many ways to identify numbers with more basic objects (sets); there is no reason to prefer one interpretation of numbers as sets to another. Nietzsche thinks science is an antidote to religious superstition. But he does not thinks scientific rationality is an end in itself. Scientific rationality leads to a neutral kind of objectivity: "The objective man is indeed a mirror . . . his mirror-soul, eternally smoothing itself out, no longer knows how to affirm or deny" (BGE 207). Objectivity is the realization that the world has no outside (TI 6:8; WP 708, 765). It is the "great liberation", that restores the "innocence of becoming" (WP 552, 765; D 13). Yet the neutrality of objectivity is not the goal. It is only a step towards positive self-reflection, to absolute affirmation.

9. From Objectivity to Self-Affirmation

Nietzsche opposes ascetic supernaturalism with his own *Dionysian naturalism*. Dionysian naturalism argues that there are only internal perspectives on the world, and that ascetic supernaturalism is in fact a self-negating and viciously circular internal perspective. It is the perspective of moral sickness, of life-hatred and world-hatred.

Dionysian naturalism "smooths rough souls and lets them taste a new desire -- to lie still as a mirror, that the deep sky may mirror itself in them" (BGE 295). Dionysian mirroring is the true self-interpretation of the world; it is not a privileged perspective, but the affirmation of every perspective. It is a perfectly accurate reflection of the world from every angle without any distorting negativity.

To the extent that any internal map is accurate, it contains a copy of itself. If any map of the world is inside the world, then it is located at some place in the world, and that place is on the map. So, located at the corresponding place on the map, there is a copy of the map. If the map is really accurate, its copy of itself contains a copy of itself. If the map is perfectly accurate, something really strange happens: it contains a copy of itself, which contains a copy of itself, and so on to infinity. Since any *true* internal map is perfectly accurate, any true internal map contains an infinite progression of copies of itself. But in this case, the copies are all perfectly identical. They are the same. Nietzsche's name for this sameness is *the eternal recurrence*. It is the perfectly true self-reflection of the world.

Dionysian naturalism releases the mind from its bondage to ascetic self-degradation: "A spirit thus *emancipated* stands in the midst of the universe with a joyful and trusting fatalism, in the *faith* that only what is separate and individual may be rejected, that in the totality everything is redeemed and affirmed -- *he no longer denies.*" (TI 9:49).

Endnotes.

1. For labyrinths, see GS 310, 322; BGE 29, 214, 295. The labyrinth is a chaos. The labyrinth is an abyss containing monsters: BGE 146.
2. Nietzsche's idea of internal conceptual maps of the world (interpretations or perspectives) anticipates the 20th Century American thinker Quine's theory of *conceptual schemes*. See W. V. Quine, "Identity, ostension, and hypostasis", in S. Hales (Ed.), *Metaphysics: Contemporary Readings*, 1st Ed. (New York: Wadsworth, 1999), pp. 461 - 468.
3. For an introduction to Putnam's internal realism, see H. Putnam, "Why there isn't a ready-made world", in S. Hales (Ed.), *Metaphysics: Contemporary Readings*, 1st Ed. (New York: Wadsworth, 1999), pp. 63 - 76.
4. Nietzsche does not worry much about possibilities; but his discussion of the infinite system of self-interpretations of the world in GS 374, his insistence on the ultimate ambiguity of existence in GS 373, his relational theory of the will to power, his theory of chance (D 130; GS 277, 288; Z 3:4, 3:16/3; WP 673) and chaos (GS 109, 322), and his arguments for recurrence (Z 3:2/2, Z 3:16/3; WP 1066) imply that he has a rich theory of possibility.
5. The world is closed in space (WP 1067). Nietzsche's theory of the eternal recurrence (GS 341; WP 1060-1067), which says that history exactly repeats itself, entails that time is a closed loop. Nietzsche's arguments that recurrence is a consequence of the complete actualization of all possible combinations of events (WP 1066; Z 3:2/2) means that the world is closed logically.
6. Nietzsche frequently discusses the opposition of this world to the other world. See TI 3:5, 3:6, 4 - 7; AC 15; WP 507, 567, 568, 570, 579, 583, 584, 586, 592.
7. Nick Herbert discusses 8 different interpretations of quantum mechanics in his *Quantum Reality: Beyond the New Physics* (New York: Doubleday, 1985).

2
Religion

1. Magical Supernaturalism

Nietzsche derives his views about religion from historical analysis (D 95). He argues that religion began as an attempt to explain the human situation. When you experience pain or pleasure, success or failure, fortune or misfortune, it is rational to seek an explanation. One explanation is that you are lucky or unlucky. The theory that luck explains your successes and failures is emotionally unappealing for several reasons. First, luck is far too abstract and mysterious to really explain anything. Second, luck is impersonal. Third, if luck is why you succeed or fail, then you are at the risk of accidents that you cannot manipulate. Luck is not emotionally satisfying.

Another explanation is that the universe (the physical or natural part of the world in which we live) is ordered by causal laws, so that actions produce effects determined by those laws. But that view isn't possible in scientifically primitive cultures, since they have no concept of natural law or causality (HH I:111; D 33; GS 86).

So, finally, primitive cultures settle on *magical explanations*. These are the basis for primitive religions. Magical explanations involve personifications. Natural forces are thought of in personal terms. Persons are *projected* into (imagined as being active in) nature. It is very hard for us to see things as things and not as people; we personify and anthropomorphize everything (AOM 26; see GS 109; TI 6:3).

If there are persons in nature, then success and failure, pleasure and pain, are relations you have with those persons. But relations among persons are moral or political relations. Fortune and misfortune now have *moral explanations*. As a child, your parents responded to your actions according to their moral code: you were rewarded by your parents for being good and punished for being bad; so, fortune is reward for your virtues and goodness, misfortune is punishment for your vices and wickedness. Parents are replaced with *spirits*. God is our *Father*. The only force one knows about is the will; so, the spirits intend us to succeed, they intended us to fail. Success is a blessing; failure is a curse. All our enterprises are evaluated morally.

Of course, fortune and misfortune are distributed in completely arbitrary ways: "The whole of nature is in the conception of religious men a sum of actions by conscious and willful beings: a tremendous complex of *arbitrariness*." (HH I:111) But instead of recognizing this as evidence against one's religious explanation, one says that the intentions of the spirits are incomprehensible to humans. This too has its origin in the relation of child to parent: the child certainly does not understand the parent's reasons for punishing or rewarding. Just so, we cannot understand the reasons of the spirits.

Magical supernaturalism projects a world of spirits behind the visible and tangible natural universe. Our relations with that spirit-world are much like our relations with the dream-world that we enter when we fall asleep. In the dream-world, things happen magically. There are no laws. We have dream-bodies with magic powers. Nietzsche says primitive humans mistook the dream-world for another reality:

> The man of the ages of barbarous primordial culture believed that in the dream he was getting to know a *second real world:* here is the origin of all metaphysics. Without the dream one would have had no occasion to divide the world into two. The dissection into soul and body is also connected with the oldest idea of the dream, likewise the postulation of a life of the soul, thus the origin of all belief in spirits. (HH I:5; but see AC 15)

So the spirit-world is developed by analogy with the dream-world. The dream-world and the spirit-world are irregular worlds ruled by arbitrary powers. We do not understand nature any more than we understand our dreams. The dream-world is also a death-world. Dying is similar to falling asleep: so perhaps when we die, we enter the spirit-world completely, and see clearly what goes on there.

At this point, the relations between the gods and humans are wholly tyrannical. The gods stand to humans as parents to children, masters to slaves, humans to animals. But since the gods are *persons*, one can treat them politically: we can try to gain their favor with bribes and gifts (offerings) or with pleas (prayers). Everything is explained by appeal to human activities. Just as husbands beat their wives and parents abuse their children, so, perhaps the gods punish those they love. If one suffers misfortune despite having made sacrifices, perhaps it is because one has sacrificed to the wrong god, or because some other god is jealous, or because the gods are at war. At this point, all moral relations are relations of friends and enemies.

2. Moral Supernaturalism

To explain human fortune and misfortune, magical supernaturalism invents a world of personal superhuman powers behind the natural world, a supernatural world populated with spirit people (who have minds and wills). During the course of cultural development, spirits become gods, gods become God. Polytheism becomes monotheism, superstition becomes philosophical. For Nietzsche, this is what is happening in ancient Greece and Rome.

In more barbaric ages, the will of the gods is purely emotional. The gods are lawless. But as human societies become more lawful, so too the arbitrary emotional will of the gods is replaced by a divine moral code. The divine moral code has some coherence: it is a reasonable order. But the order is merely conventional: the gods or spirits have a legal system, in which humans are on trial in a divine court to be punished or rewarded. But the divine legal system is still a political system in which the gods are open to *persuasion:* deals can be made, perhaps the god can be bribed with a new temple or a sacrifice.

Polytheism is more life-affirming than monotheism (GS 143). As Greco-Roman polytheism gives way to Judeo-Christian monotheism, the multiple moral conventions of the gods turns into the absolute moral commandments of God. The flexible morality that was open to persuasion becomes an inflexible rule: a standard of moral perfection against which all human actions are measured. After death, we will be rewarded for how well we measure up to the standard, punished for how poorly we measure up to it. Since the divine moral code is the standard of goodness, the supernatural world, the disembodied world of fleshless souls, is invested with all positive values.

3. Ascetic Supernaturalism

Since the supernatural world is invested with all positive values, and since primitive logic thinks in terms of pairs of opposites, the natural world is divested of all positive values: only negative values are left in it. Primitive logic reasons (erroneously) that opposites have to be lined up with one another, and that the positive cannot emerge from the negative. (HH I:1; GS 111; BGE 2; TI 3:4) The Pythagoreans, for in-

13

stance, came up with a table of ten opposites: good / evil, male / female, light / dark, left / right, and so on.

So the religious mind reasons like this: natural and supernatural are opposites; good and evil are opposites; if supernatural is good, then natural must be evil. The natural world is devoid of all goodness. It is the evil, false, illusory, ugly world. The supernatural world is the good, true, real, beautiful world. Alternatively, the earth is kind of a *neutral* place suspended between a good heaven and an evil hell. So the earth isn't even evil: it's *valueless*.

Asceticism is the *love* of the supernatural world plus the *hatred* of the natural world. Asceticism hates the earth, hates the body, hates life, hates sex. But since ascetics are humans who live on the earth and who have bodies and who have sexual desires, asceticism is a kind of self-loathing, self-hatred, self-negation. Ascetics are not active. Ascetics turn their action inward against themselves, so they are *reactive*. (GM 2:11-12) Ascetics are people who cannot "rid themselves of self-loathing, hatred of the earth and of all living things, who inflict as much pain as possible on themselves, solely out of pleasure in giving pain -- perhaps the only kind of pleasure they know." (GM 3:11) Asceticism is a kind of sterile masochism.

4. Religious Supernaturalism and Asceticism

Nietzsche doesn't hate religion. He hates religious supernaturalism and asceticism. Supernaturalism says the other world is not natural; the other world is anti-natural. Asceticism adds that all value exists in the other world; so, the natural world has no value: it is worthless.

Nietzsche doesn't think ascetic supernaturalism is totally negative. Its a perspective on the world (and human life in the world) from within the world (TI 5:5). Although it pretends to see the world from an external point of view, it's really an internal point of view. No internal perspective is absolutely negative. For if any internal perspective is absolutely negative, it refutes itself. Nietzsche finds something positive even in ascetic supernaturalism (GM 3:13): it's the perspective adopted by spiritually sick people or cultures that are either in the process of self-destruction or recuperation. Ascetic supernaturalism does refute itself, either by suicide or recovery.

5. Opposition to Christianity

Nietzsche thinks that supernaturalism and asceticism come together most intensely in Christianity. Nietzsche acknowledges that

Christianity has some positive effects; but he thinks that, on the whole, Christianity is negative. Instead of offering effective solutions to people who are suffering, it offers the narcotic illusion of heaven. Christianity is negative mainly because it denies the truth, reality, and goodness of life in this world -- on the actual earth in the physical universe. Instead, it affirms the existence and value of a *supernatural* world of spirits or souls. The spirit-world is defined negatively, as unnatural and anti-natural, like an inverted mirror-image or photographic negative of nature. Christianity tries to get people to hate nature, the earth, and the body by insisting that the spirit-world is the true, real, and good world, so this world is false, illusory, and evil.

Worst of all, Christianity sets up an opposition in the spirit-world between heaven and hell, so that we fear hell and hope for heaven. Consequently, we fall under the real social and political control of the priests in this world. Christianity may be a fantasy, but when people act out of Christian beliefs their real actions have real consequences.

Christians believe the world will end in an apocalyptic earth-destroying battle between good and evil. A Christian waiting for the apocalypse in a cave in the desert is simply foolish. A Christian nation that believes in the apocalypse, and that controls enough nuclear weapons to wipe out all life on earth, is dangerous.

6. Christ versus Christianity

Surprisingly, Nietzsche has a very positive attitude to Christ. He thinks Christianity perverts Christ's own teachings: "What did Christ *deny?* Everything that today is called Christian" (WP 158); "The church is precisely that against which Jesus preached -- and against which he taught his disciples to fight" (WP 168); "Christians have never put into practice the acts Jesus prescribed for them" (WP 191); "What is wrong with Christianity is that it refrains from doing all those things that Christ commanded should be done" (WP 193).

Nietzsche thinks of Jesus as a sort of revolutionary, a "holy anarchist" who set out to overthrow the Jewish priesthood (AC 27). Jesus says that true eternal life is "here, it is within you: as life lived in love, in love without deduction or exclusion" (AC 29).[1] Nietzsche says Jesus "never had any reason to deny 'the world' . . . *Denial* is precisely what is totally impossible for him" (AC 32). Nietzsche presents Jesus as a free spirit, as an affirmative person (AC 27-35), and even says that Christ is "the noblest human being" (HH I:475). He portrays Jesus as beyond good and evil: "Jesus said to his Jews: 'The law was for servants -- love God as I love him, as his son! What are morals to us sons of God!'" (BGE 164).

The perversion of Christ's teachings was carried out by St. Paul, the Church Fathers, and St. Augustine: "Paul re-erected on a grand scale precisely that which Christ had annulled through his way of living" (WP 167). Much of Nietzsche's anti-Christianity is an opposition to Paul's perversion of it (D 68). Indeed, Nietzsche declares that "God, as Paul created him, is a denial of God" (AC 47). Paul transforms Christ's joyful wisdom into an anti-worldly asceticism (GS 139; AC 58). Through Paul, *profound* hatred of the world enters religion. In the modern era, Nietzsche thinks Luther, the 16th Century German who founded Protestantism, carries on this hatred (GS 148).

7. Christian Ascetic Supernaturalism

The theory that the supernatural world contains all *real* value (both positive and negative) leads Christianity to declare that it is a world of *compensation.* God's justice makes up for all injustices suffered by Christians on earth (and all misfortunes are injustices according to the supernaturalism). The misfortunes the Christian suffers on this earth are merely apparent; they are illusions. But soon God will *really* reward and *really* punish. Unable to succeed on earth, the Christian will be rewarded in heaven. Unable to get revenge on earth, the Christian will get compensatory revenge in heaven.

Nietzsche cites a passage from Tertullian (one of the Fathers of the Christian church), in which Tertullian describes the sadistic pleasures the Christians in heaven will have as they watch the Romans who persecuted them being tortured in hell. (GM 1:15) Tertullian's vicious cruelty is remarkable. Nietzsche stresses this vengeful aspect of Christianity. He thinks it is a religion of *hate*, not love.

According to Christianity, all the things that bind us to this world are evil -- especially sex, which makes us love not some fantastic god but real people, and not their souls, but their bodies. Sex leads to a concern for the future of one's children in this world, not for the future of one's soul in the supernatural world. But, as St. Augustine discovered, the sexual drive can be made sick. It is not so much chastity that is at issue, but the attitude that motivates it. On Nietzsche's view, puritanical hatred of sexuality is itself a sexual perversion.

8. Philosophical Ascetic Supernaturalism

As much as he accuses Christianity for its asceticism, Nietzsche also accuses philosophy. The ascetic corruption of the mind starts with Parmenides, who says all change is an illusion (PTG 9). Socrates continues the corruption (TI 2). Socrates corrupts Plato (GS 372). Of all the ancient thinkers, only Heraclitus remains innocent. One of the most ascetic of ancient philosophers is the Roman thinker Plotinus. Plotinus's writings are collected together in a book called the *Enneads*. According to Plotinus: "life in the body is of itself an evil" (*Enneads* I.7.3.20-23); "the soul is evil by being interfused with the body" (I.2.3; I.6.6). We ought to take the same attitude toward our earthly bodies that a gardener takes to the maggots in the rotten part of a plant (IV.3.4.29-33);[2] "Life here, with the things of earth, is a sinking, a defeat, a failing of the wing" (VI.9.9). Since bodily life on earth is evil, our goal is to escape from the world: "Since evil is here . . . and it is the Soul's design to escape from Evil, we must escape from here" (I.2.1; III.6.6) our goal is "liberation from the alien that besets us here, a life taking no pleasure in the things of earth" (VI.9.9-11). As far as Nietzsche is concerned, such asceticism is simply sickness. Far from being spiritually good, it is spiritually bad. Asceticism is an illness, it is a disease of the human spirit.

9. Scientific Supernaturalism

With the emergence of science, people realize that the causal order behind nature is not a moral order, but a mathematical order. The world has no moral order (D 563; TI 7:1; WP 258). The divine standard is not moral. Moral action has no effect on natural forces. For instance, religious rituals (e.g. prayers and sacrifices) do not influence the weather or health or the economy or war.

Science declares that the world-order is impersonally mechanistic, not spiritual. If you get sick and you want to get well, you should go to a doctor, not a priest. You should take medicine, not pray. Prayer may have a positive effect, but that is due to human emotion, not God. Technology is effective; magical religious rituals are not. Human fortunes and misfortunes are explained by chance -- accidents, not miracles. Mathematics is not personal. Science explains nature in a way that is as effective as it is inhuman and non-moral.

While science seems to be against supernaturalism, its naturalism isn't fully affirmative. Science doesn't totally get rid of the supernatural world, since it has a faith of its own. The supernatural world for science is populated by theoretical entities and forces, like atoms and gravity. These are biologically useful fictions; they do not exist (GS 112, 121). Scientific materialism is a kind of ascetic faith:

> those who are truthful in that audacious and ultimate sense that is presupposed by the faith in science *thus affirm another world* than

the world of life, nature, and history; and insofar as they affirm this "other world" -- look, must they not by the same token negate its counter part, this world, *our* world? -- it is still a *metaphysical faith* upon which our faith in science rests . . . the faith of Plato, that God is truth, that truth is divine. (GS 344, 373)

The essential change is that the supernatural world is not a moral or emotional world. The religious priest is replaced by the scientific priest. Scientific priests have faith in science. Often, their faith has the same structure as the Christian faith before it.

For example, consider the 20th century American physicist Frank Tipler, who wrote a book titled *The Physics of Immortality: Modern Cosmology, God and the Resurrection of the Dead*.[3] Tipler wants to use technology to make a future that conforms to Christian ascetic values. Or consider the 20th century American robotics scientist Hans Moravec,[4] who thinks of the soul as a mathematical program and describes the resurrection of the body as a robot (your mind is copied from your brain and put into a robotic body). Moravec is a true ascetic. He talks approvingly of the divorce of the mind from the body.[5] The human body is evil. Tipler gets most of his ideas from Moravec, but both get their ideas from St. Paul. Only ascetic values could lead to the development of weapons of mass destruction, the tools with which the Christian Apocalypse might be made real.

Scientific supernaturalism, despite its Christian themes, isn't quite the same. The supernatural world in which one invested emotional values (one's hope for heaven and fear of hell) is sterilized. It is still personal, but its personality is coldly rational. God becomes an emotionless calculating super-mind, not a caring deity. Scientific supernaturalism quickly leads to nihilism. Stripped of its emotional warmth, the supernatural world becomes as sterile as it is empty.

10. The Death of the Christian God

Nietzsche says that God is dead (GS 108, 125, 343; BGE 55). He's not the first to say it. Ralph Waldo Emerson, the 19th century American thinker, said that "Men have come to speak of the revelation as something long ago given and done, as if God were dead."[6]

When Nietzsche says that God is dead, he means that the theory of God we are most familiar with, the Christian-Platonic theory of God, isn't true because it doesn't describe anything real. It doesn't even make sense. He denies the existence of anything corresponding to the Christian-Platonic God. He denies *theism*. (HH I:25, I:28, I:245;

AOM 225; BGE 53)

Theism says something like this: God is some one, eternal, personal, all-powerful, intelligent, all-knowing, truthful, morally good, caring, purposive, supreme being. You can add conscious, male, and triune if you like. Nietzsche denies that there is any such God. You might say that Nietzsche is an atheist. Lots of people say that. I think it's more accurate to say that Nietzsche denies the Christian-Platonic theory of God than that he denies the existence of anything divine. Nietzsche himself is very suspicious about atheism. He says: "The Christian moral God is not tenable: hence 'atheism' -- as if there could be no other kinds of god" (WP 151, 1005). The distinction between theism and atheism is a Christian invention anyway. The Christians say: either our God or no God. But you don't have to believe in Christianity to believe in God. You can deny Christianity altogether and nevertheless believe in God. In that case, you just don't believe in the Christian God. You can be anti-Christ and anti-Christian without being anti-God. That's an important point for anybody who is religious but not Christian. Christianity is not the only religion, the Christian God is not the only God.

Saying Nietzsche is an atheist simplifies his thought to the point of triviality. It stereotypes his philosophy. As happens all too often, Nietzsche's powerful but strange concepts are forced into familiar categories. If you know that he's an atheist, then you really don't have to bother to *think* about what he says about God. Instead of saying he's an atheist, I prefer to say that Nietzsche's philosophy is *transtheism*. In transtheism "trans" means beyond or after. Transtheism isn't theism or atheism. Transtheism denies the opposition of theism to atheism.

Nietzsche does not so much want to deny the existence of God as to redeem us from the use to which God has been put. So far, God has been used "to darken the heavens, to blot out the sun, to cast suspicion on joy, to deprive hope of its value, to paralyze the active hand" (D 41). Asceticism has infected God with hate; Nietzsche declares that we must cleanse "even God of this filth" (WP 765).

11. Nihilism

In nihilism, the opposition of natural to supernatural remains, even though the supernatural world is lost. The nihilist reasons (wrongly) like this: the home of the good values is gone, so those values must be gone too. One used to love heaven and hate the earth, now one cannot love heaven, since there is no heaven, but one can still hate the earth. One can hate it even more for having destroyed heaven.

According to Nietzsche, ascetic Christianity is like alcohol or

19

heroin. It is a narcotic anti-depressant (GS 147; WP 30). Like other drugs, Christianity is addictive. Our culture has been addicted for 2000 years. Nihilism is the hangover, the agonizing withdrawal. Nihilism can be active: the nihilist seeks revenge against the earth for the loss of heaven. Or nihilism can be passive. The nihilist has lost his or her compensation for misfortune, so that misfortunes are no longer *meaningful*. The nihilist has lost a great source of comfort, hope, and means to emotionally endure life on this earth. So the nihilist hates the earth even more, for now he or she is in pain, and there is no narcotic. The nihilist still needs a savior, still needs a cure, since one is still sick. So he or she looks for salvation in other places: in art (Romanticism), in scientific progress, or the Revolution (so, messianic socialism is a version of Christian nihilism; TI 9:34). Perhaps the nihilist will find salvation in the human spirit or in his or her own self (existentialism, secular humanism). What Nietzsche wants is for the nihilist to overcome asceticism: to stop denying this world, this earth, this body, this life; to get over his or her addiction; to say Yes! to life.

12. Buddhism

A religion like Buddhism is able to help the nihilist away from his or her addiction to asceticism. Nietzsche has an extremely positive attitude towards Buddhism, which he often opposes to Christianity. He thinks that Buddhism is a pessimistic religion, that it is nihilistic. But he also thinks it is free from the absurd dogmas and ascetic supernaturalism of Christianity. Despite it's pessimism, Buddhism is clearheaded and sober. Despite its nihilism, it is a *noble* religion:

> Buddhism is a hundred times more realistic than Christianity -- it has the heritage of a cool and objective posing of problems . . . the concept 'God' is already abolished by the time it arrives. Buddhism is the only really positivistic religion history has to show us . . . It already has -- and this distinguishes it profoundly from Christianity -- the self-deception of moral concepts behind it -- it stands, in my language, beyond good and evil. (AC 20)

Nevertheless, Nietzsche is not a Buddhist and does not advertise for Buddhism or want to convert you to it. Buddhism is nihilistic, and what Nietzsche wants is an affirmative religious attitude.

13. Opposition to Nihilistic Religion

Nietzsche is not opposed to the existence of the divine. He does not deny the divine. Quite the contrary, he has a theory of divinity that is sophisticated and subtle. What he denies is the Christian God, in particular the God advanced by St. Paul in the New Testament:

> What sets us apart is not that we recognize no God, either in history or in nature or behind nature -- but that we find that which has been reverenced as God not 'godlike' but pitiable, absurd, harmful, not merely an error but a crime against life . . . God, as Paul created him, is a denial of God. (AC 47)

According to Nietzsche the Christian concept of God is both logically and morally incoherent. It is a corrupt conception of God:

> The Christian conception of God -- God as God of the sick, God as spider, God as spirit -- is one of the most corrupt conceptions of God arrived at on earth: perhaps it even represents the low-water mark in the descending development of the God type. God degenerated to the contradiction of life, instead of being its transfiguration and eternal Yes! (AC 18)

Nietzsche doesn't just attack the Christian theory of God. He has something positive to replace the Christian God. He has a Dionysian theory of divinity, although that theory doesn't have any deity. He summarizes his whole philosophy in the slogan: "Dionysus versus the Crucified" (WP 1052; EH 15:9). Dionysus is an old Greek and Roman pagan god. Dionysus is a visceral divinity; Dionysus is the divinity of the flesh. Nietzsche says that "pagans are all who say Yes to life, to whom 'God' is the word for the great Yes to all things" (AC 55).

Nothing could be worse than thinking that Nietzsche wants people to worship Dionysus. Dionysus does not exist. Nietzsche does not want us to set up Dionysus on the *throne* of the old dead God. Getting rid of God is easy; getting rid of the throne of God, the place occupied by God in your thought and action, is much much harder. You could put almost anything in the place of God: you could put humanity, morality, the universe, or your own ego there. You could even let the throne be empty and treat *nothingness* as if it were God (BGE 55). But you can't put Dionysus on the throne because Dionysus isn't a god or even a thing. Dionysus is a *way of life*. Dionysus is *Yes!*

14. Alternatives to Ascetic Supernaturalism

For Nietzsche, the ultimate philosophical problem is the problem of human suffering, the problem of human fortune and misfortune, success and failure, moral pleasure and moral pain. Nietzsche knows very well that the passage of time will destroy everything that is valuable to every one of us: it will destroy our bodies, our lovers, our families. It will destroy those we love most.

There are many responses to the problem of human suffering. One is ascetic supernaturalism: the denial and hatred of the natural world and the affirmation and love of an illusory anti-natural world, the demand for compensation for one's suffering and misfortune. A second response to the problem of human suffering is *detachment*. One refuses to have any emotional participation or involvement in this world. This is the Buddhist or Epicurean response. Since these deny the world of change, Nietzsche does not like them. But he does say they are much better responses than ascetic supernaturalism.

A third response is Stoicism. The Stoics were ancient Greek and Roman philosophers who taught that tranquillity or equanimity is the ideal moral state. Equanimity (*apatheia*) is a state in which one does not pass judgment on one's feelings. It is a morally neutral state. Nietzsche thinks this is better than detachment, and he recommends it as a kind of stepping-stone to his own idea of affirmation. Here's an affirmative passage from Marcus Aurelius, the Stoic philosopher who was also the Roman Emperor:

> Be like the headland against which the waves break and break: it stands firm, until presently the watery tumult around it subsides once more to rest. 'How unlucky I am, that this should have happened to me!' By no means; say rather, 'How lucky I am, that it has left me with no bitterness; unshaken by the present, and undismayed by the future.' The thing could have happened to anyone, but not everyone would have emerged unembittered. So why put the one down to misfortune, rather than the other to good fortune? . . . So here is a rule to remember in the future, when anything tempts you to feel bitter: not, 'This is a misfortune,' but 'To bear this worthily is good fortune.'[7]

15. Absolute Affirmation

Nietzsche's own response to the problem of suffering is the absolute affirmation of everything that occurs. The ultimate moral principle of existence is affirmation: *it is better to exist than not to exist.* Say Yes to every possibility, affirm every destiny. Instead of affirming some supernatural world, Nietzsche says that we ought to affirm this world. This is *religious naturalism.* Nietzsche thinks that ancient Greek religion came close to naturalism. Instead of denying our lives, our bodies, our sexualities, our earth, we ought to affirm our lives, our bodies, our sexualities, our earth. We ought to affirm our *destinies.* His name for it is *amor fati:* love of fate. His name for religious naturalism plus amor fati is *Dionysus.*[8]

Nietzsche thinks we ought to affirm everything that happens to us, no matter how pleasurable or painful. We ought to affirm "without subtraction, exception, or selection" (WP 1041). Affirmation is not a feeling or an emotional reaction. Affirmation has nothing to do with feeling. Affirmation is a *moral judgment:* you affirm regardless of what you feel. Nietzsche thinks that we ought to affirm what feels good as well as what feels bad. *Feelings are not moral facts.*

You can feel angry without being angry. You can be happy without feeling happy. You can be affirmative while suffering the agonies of hell. Suffering is passive; affirmation is active. Nietzsche's insight is that our feelings do not entitle us to make moral judgments. The opposite of affirmation is *condemnation.* Just because something hurts us, just because we suffer, we are not thereby entitled to condemn the world or to demand compensation.

Instead of a compensatory metaphysical theory (which is a fantasy of revenge on life), Nietzsche develops a metaphysical theory that says that history repeats itself on a grand scale. He argues that we will live again -- but not in any other world. We will return to our lives as human animals in our own bodies on this earth, because the history of the universe repeats itself. This is his notion of eternal recurrence. It is a kind of resurrection without any judgment, reward, or punishment.

Nietzsche encourages egocentric hopes that are worldly -- faith in this world, this earth, this body. The eternal return is such a faith: your compensation is here on this earth with this body. The eternal return is faith in the immortality of the flesh. Hope for something only insofar as you can argue for it (EH 5:2). The eternal return is an affirmative faith that is friendly to truth. Let the will to truth drive all your hopes to Yes.

Endnotes.

1. The notion of resurrection (which is not originally Christian, but becomes a central doctrine of Christianity) is in many respects world-affirming and life-affirming: it affirms the life of the flesh on

earth, not the abstract existence of any disembodied soul in an other world. Nietzsche's idea of eternal recurrence predicts the resurrection of the body. It is a Dionysian resurrection.

2. See S. R. L. Clark, "Plotinus: Body and Soul" in L. P. Gerson (ed.) *The Cambridge Companion to Plotinus* (Cambridge: Cambridge University Press, 1996), pp. 275-291; for maggots, see. p. 284 & p. 289.

3. F. Tipler, *The Physics of Immortality: Modern Cosmology, God and the Resurrection of the Dead* (New York: Doubleday, 1994).

4. H. Moravec, *Mind Children: The Future of Robot and Human Intelligence* (Cambridge, MA: Harvard University Press, 1988), especially ch. 4.

5. H. Moravec, "The Coming Divorce in Human Nature", *Whole Earth Review 63* (Summer 1989), p. 13; see also G. J. Sussman, "Is the Body Obsolete?", *Whole Earth Review 63*, p. 16.

6. R. W. Emerson, "The Divinity School Address," in *Selected Essays, Lectures, and Poems* (New York: Bantam Books, 1990), p. 115.

7. Marcus Aurelius, *Meditations*, Bk. 4, 49.

8. Nietzsche identifies this plentitude with Dionysus: TI 3:6, 9:49, 10:4-5; EH 5:1-3, 10:6-8; WP 1019, 1041.

3

Knowledge

1. The Evolution of Cognition

Nietzsche takes Darwin seriously when it comes to kinowledge and cognition. Cognition evolves. Crystals exhibit pre-cognitive abilities insofar as they extend their own patterns into the molten flux that surrounds them (WP 499; PT 110, p. 39). Living cells extend their own patterns into other material as they incorporate nutrients. Such extension is cognitive insofar as it equalizes the unequal and transforms the other into the same (WP 500, 510, 511). Evolutionary forces drive organisms to become more and more complex, and their cognitive abilities increasing in complexity along with their bodies.

The most basic cognitive operations originate far back in the evolutionary chain. Plants have primitive stimulus-response reflexes and primitive memories (PT 97 p. 36, 101 p. 37; WP 544). To the plant "every thing is identical with itself. It is from the period of the lower organisms that man has inherited the belief that there are *identical things*." (HH I:18)

As cognition evolves, living physical systems that are parts of the universe become more and more aware of their surroundings. This evolutionary progress climaxes in human self-consciousness, in which part of the universe is aware of the whole of which it is a part. Human animals are those parts of the whole that mirror the whole (PT 102 p. 37-38; see HH I:2, I:10, I:16).

The human mind does not mirror the universe from outside it, from any "God's-Eye View", since the human mind evolved from inside the world and mirrors it from the inside. Of course, as it mirrors the whole world more clearly and completely, as its knowledge gets truer and truer, it must also mirror itself. If its mirroring becomes absolutely accurate, so that the mirror perfectly reflects the whole, then it also becomes an infinitely self-nested series of reflections.

2. Truth versus Utility

Insofar as any part of the universe mirrors the whole universe, it does so from some perspective. What justifies the "truth" of the perspective of any evolved part on the whole is that its perspective has facilitated its evolution. The perspectives that evolve are the ones that are useful for their own evolution.

Nietzsche says that "for a particular species to maintain itself and increase its power, its conception of reality must comprehend enough of the calculable and constant for it to base a scheme of behavior on it" (WP 480). Such calculability is the "truth" for that species. So: "For the plant, the whole world is a plant; for us, it is human" (PT 102 p. 38). Indeed, Nietzsche suspects it is almost impossible for a person to see things impersonally, to see them as things and not as people (AOM 26). We anthropomorphize non-human reality: we explain the operations of non-human things just like we explain the behaviors of people. Why did the storm destroy our crops? Because the sky-god is angry with us. But why is the sky-god angry with us? Because we have offended him. Natural phenomena are explained in terms of emotions (anger) and moral reactions (offense). Nietzsche says that our adoption of this human perspective does not stop with the development of advanced abstract formal science (HH I:37).

Our human perspective was biologically successful and thrived, while others did not. While there may be perspectives that are "truer" than ours in some ultimate sense, the organisms that were evolving those truer perspectives have not survived to adopt them (GS 111). So those truer perspectives are self-defeating: so far they have not proven, at least on earth, that they are able to exist, so their truth negates itself. Since every perspective on the universe is taken from some context in it, truth as it actually realizes itself is limited by contextual utility -- there are no perspectives that are more true than they are useful. Any perspective that is truer than it is useful dies out.

Our "truths" are no more than articles of faith without which we are not able to live. All human knowledge (including our most advanced scientific and mathematical knowledge) is no more than a system of propositions consistent with those propositions without which human animals like us could not survive (GS 110). If we say a proposition is true, then we mean only that it is consistent with our life-preserving errors: "What are man's truths ultimately? Merely his irrefutable errors"

(GS 265); "Truth is the kind of error without which a species of life could not live" (WP 493); "Truths are illusions which we have forgotten are illusions" (PT p. 84).

Nietzsche now makes an argument whose cold-blooded rationality is deeply disturbing: he says "Life is no argument" (GS 121). He says "the conditions of life might include error" (GS 121). This argument provides him with a method: he searches for our most basic articles of faith, the ones humans have affirmed as absolutely true, and he will treat them as if they were errors. This is skepticism (HH I:21). Nietzsche is skeptical like Sextus Empiricus, Descartes, and Hume. Since the truth of any proposition is limited by its contextual utility, it is always possible that any proposition is absolutely false.

3. Life-Preserving Errors

Nietzsche provides a detailed catalog of articles of faith of which he is skeptical. The long list of errors includes: that there are identical or equal things (GS 110, 111; HH I:11, I:18, I:19, I:286, WS 11); that things are self-identical over time (HH I:11, I:18) that there are enduring things (GS 110, 112); that there is an ego (BGE 12, 17, 19); that there is free will (HH I: 39; AOM 50; BGE 18, 19, 21); that there are causes and effects (GS 112, 121; BGE 21; WP 545-552, 554, 617); that there are abstract mathematical objects like points, lines, planes or theoretical scientific objects like atoms, units of time, units of space (GS 112, 121); that there are natural laws (AOM 9); that what is what is good for me is good in itself (GS 110); that humans are superior to animals and to nature (GS 113); that human moral systems are eternal that there is an absolute right and wrong (GS 113); that there is another world besides this one (GS 151).

4. The Fictions of Identity and Equality

Perception equalizes its experiences; it blurs stimuli and groups them together into fictitious units on the basis of similarity. Animals that do not treat similar stimuli as equal by ignoring the details must do more cognitive processing of stimuli to produce their behaviors; so they are slower, so they fail to get food and fail to avoid predators; so they are less likely to survive and to have offspring, despite the fact that perceptual cognition is truer (GS 111). The perceptual error of equating similars and reacting identically has greater survival value, so evolution by natural selection reinforces this error.

False perception produces concepts by blurring unique individuals together into a single abstract mental image, the concept:

Every concept arises from the equation of unequal things. Just as it is certain that one leaf is never totally the same as another, so it is certain that the concept "leaf" is formed by arbitrarily discarding these individual differences and by forgetting the distinguishing aspects. . . . We obtain the concept, as we do the form, by overlooking what is individual (PT, p. 83)

The emergence of concepts through erroneous identification or false equalization leads to the erection of the conceptual world over the perceptual world. Concepts are then projected outside of the mind, so the projector affirms the existence of abstract objects: the Platonic Forms. The forms are thought of as unchanging and eternal. Since the forms are changeless, any true theory of forms is absolutely true, perfectly reliable and useful. The world of forms becomes the true world. The conceptualization of the body, and the false projection of that concept as a real form, leads to the idea of the immortal soul. So the conceptual world is the place of eternal life, where no action is ever frustrated by unreliable knowledge and where nothing of value is ever lost due to destruction. The true world is paradise. Nietzsche, of course, thinks this is superstition: illusion and self-delusion. But it all has its roots in the fictions of equality and identity.

5. The Self-Interpretation of Thought

Nietzsche thinks that the two deepest errors of identity and equality emerge from the self-interpretation of thought. Nietzsche argues like this: identity and equality are common to all thought; since the content of thought always varies, all that is constant in all thought is the relation of thought to itself; so, any error common to all thought is an error of its self-interpretation.

For Nietzsche, thought is mysterious to itself, since any true thought about thinking leads to an infinite regress -- for that thought has to think about itself thinking about itself, and so on, like a mirror reflecting itself. The eye is not able to see itself in the act of its vision: for if it ever does that, it only ends up seeing itself seeing itself seeing . . . Since that endless regress never reaches any visible object, nothing is seen. Vision is invisible; thought is unthinkable. It is mysterious to itself.

To avoid the infinite regress of pure self-awareness, thought has to think of itself *as if it were another* -- as if it were not itself. Thought is at most able to catch a glimpse of itself indirectly. As it tries to make sense out of itself, thought projects that indirect glimpse of itself into itself. Its self-image is the result of an interpretative process through which it regularizes and organizes its own activities, reducing "the multiplicity of its processes" to a fictitious unity -- the ego. Furthermore, it projects this ego into itself, as the active agent responsible for the production of psychic processes: thought has no clue what really is doing the thinking, but as it directs itself to itself it becomes aware of something -- so it declares that what it becomes aware of is itself as an object of thought: the soul or ego or "I". The ego is the original object, for it is the original object of thought, so all other objects of thought are modelled on the ego. Thought thinks of its objectified activity as an enduring self-identical thing.

Thought thinks that the ego causes thought, that the ego has the power to make thought happen. Thought thinks that this power is the will. It says that the ego is an object that wills, and that the will is the force that causes the body to move. Of course, this power to move the body is utterly mysterious to thought: you are not able to move your arm just by thinking about moving your arm any more than you are able to move a rock just by thinking about moving it. Through its own self-interpretation, thought posits two fictions: mental substance (ego) and mental force (will).

When thought turns to the interpretation of the chaos of sensation occurring in it, it utilizes its self-image narcissistically as the basis of its interpretation of that chaos. As it interprets the chaos happening in itself, thought projects its own self-image (ego and will, object and force) into that chaos of stimuli. Humans project their thoughts:

> Man projected his three 'inner facts', that in which he believed more firmly than in anything else, will, spirit, ego, outside himself -- he derived the concept 'being' only from the concept 'ego', he posited 'things' as possessing being according to his own image, according to his concept of the ego as cause. (TI 6:3)

As it projects its self-image into the chaos of stimuli, thought makes a mirror-image of itself on the other side of appearances -- and it is an error of vision that appearances have an other side. A fictitious material substance or thing-in-itself is projected into experience as the hidden cause of its experience.

Thought sets up the subject/object split in itself with itself in the middle, projecting an unknowable ego as the cause of its experience on the subjective side, and an unknowable material thing or thing-in-itself as the cause of its experience on the objective side.

6. The Projection of the Ego and the Will

From the fiction of the ego, thinking or reason derives the fiction of things. Using the ego as a model, thought projects the fiction of an enduring, self-identical thing into the chaos of sensations: "It is only after the model of the subject that we have invented the reality of things and projected them into the medley of sensations"(WTP 552). Thought affirms that there is an objective external world of material substances, things-in-themselves, or atoms, and that the things in the external world cause the sensations it experiences. Thought *"projects* its beliefs in the ego-substance on to all things -- only thus does it *create* the concept 'thing' . . . . Being is everywhere thought in, *foisted on*, as cause; it is only from the conception 'ego' that there follows, derivatively, the concept 'being'." (TI 3:5).

Likewise, "We believed ourselves to be causal agents in the act of willing" (TI 6:3); but that is an error. The fiction of mental force is then externalized as mechanical force, so that the external world of material objects is a world of projected egos interacting by projected wills. This whole objective world is, according to Nietzsche, nothing more than a false anthropomorphism. It is an externalized human society, so that even the most abstract science unconsciously adds moral value judgments and social conventions to its theories.

7. The Fiction of Substances

The ego is a single, unitary thing. The Christian-Platonic name for this ego is "soul." The soul, according to Christian Platonism, is an atom (BGE 12). The physical atom is the externalization or projection of the soul atom outside of thought into the chaos of sensations. But the soul atom is an erroneous self-interpretation; so the physical atom is the projected version of an error (TI 6:3).

In positing atoms as causes operating behind the phenomena, the scientist still affirms the superstitious animistic belief that there are spirits or persons behind phenomena. The belief in atoms is still an anthropomorphization, so that the world behind phenomena, the objective world, is just a projected version of the subjective world. It is a projected version of the scientist's own self-image, and it is just as much a religious picture of the world as were earlier, more explicitly anthropomorphic interpretations or perspectives. The world picture of materialistic physics "differs in no essential way from the subjective world picture: it is only construed with more extended senses, but with *our* senses nonetheless" (WTP 636).

But the materialistic atom, like the spiritual atom (the soul), is an illusion. It was posited to satisfy an emotional need (BGE 12), a need for constant causes. The physical atom is a conventional fiction (WTP 624, 636). But materialistic atomism isn't the only physical theory going. Nietzsche was interested in the theories of the 18th Century scientist Boscovitch, who thought of the world as a network of energy-relations. Thanks to Boscovitch, we can neutralize our superstitious beliefs in atoms and enduring physical things (BGE 12). Boscovitch's ideas inspired much of the early work in quantum mechanics.

8. The Fiction of Causality

While cause and effect seem like very useful and obviously true ideas, they're very difficult to pin down precisely -- so difficult that many philosophers deny that there really are causes or effects in nature. The 18th Century British philosopher Hume is most famous for his denial of causality. Nietzsche agrees with Hume that causality is a fiction (WP 550; GS 112); but he argues further that it is derived from the belief that the will is a force. Causality is the projection of an inner illusion outside of the ego into the sensory chaos.

Primitive people thought all changes were produced by personal beings, so every event is the will of some person (GS 127). All relations between persons (souls or egos) are relations of will; so all relations between projected souls (atoms) are relations of projected will. The projected version of the will is cause and effect. Thus the scientific world view, the view that phenomena are atoms attracted or repelled by forces, is simply a projected version of the old superstitious religious view that all things are persons (egos) and that the only force is will.

The belief in the will, according to Nietzsche, is an illusion. It is another one of the self-misinterpretations of thought, it is a psychological fiction: "The 'inner world' is full of phantoms and false lights: the will is one of them. The will no longer moves anything, consequently no longer explains anything." (TI 6:3). Therefore, cause and effect are no more than conventional fictions:

One should not wrongly reify 'cause' and 'effect,' as the natural scientists do (and whoever, like them, now 'naturalizes' his thinking), according to the prevailing mechanical doltishness which makes the cause press and push until it 'effects' its end; one should use 'cause' and 'effect' only as pure concepts, that is to say, as conventional fictions for the purpose of designation and communication -- *not* for explanation. (BGE 21)

Nietzsche ultimately argues that (1) things are projections of the human ego; (2) forces are projections of the human will; (3) God is the projection of the magnified human ego; (4) the will of God is the projection of the magnified human will. So, in accordance with the superstitious perspective of animistic religion, we project magnified psychological errors (ego and will) into the universe, and therefore we imagine a human society behind the natural phenomena.

9. Regularities and Laws of Nature

The unconscious regularization of stimuli produces the illusion of the *recurrence of identical cases*. The unconscious mind does not pay attention to detail; it blurs distinctions, so that it looks like the same sequence repeats itself. The mind learns the rule lightning-thunder because it abstracts from all particular occurrences of lightning and thunder. This abstraction renders the course of events calculable: "The *calculability of an event . . .* resides in the *recurrence of 'identical cases'*" (WTP 551).[1] Recurrent identical cases are fictions that thought projects into its experiences by equalizing the unequal; so, regularities and abstract mathematical (calculable) rules are fictions too.

The fact that an event occurs in as it does happen, or is associated with another event, does not allow us to posit a law: "'Regularity' in succession is only a metaphorical expression, as if a rule were being followed here; not a fact. In the same way "conformity with a law." We discover a formula by which to express an ever-recurring kind of result: we have therewith discovered no "law," even less a force that is the cause of the recurrence of a succession of results." (WTP 632)

Few scientific concepts betray their anthropomorphic basis as much the "laws of nature." Laws are social conventions. If we think that the objects posited by physical theories obey laws, we are thinking of them as if they were human egos with free wills obeying the will of a legislating ruler (AOM 9). Natural laws are superstitions.

Behind the fiction of natural laws lies the fiction of the supreme ruling ego whose will is omnipotent: God. Any science that uses the fiction of the laws of nature is stuck in magical theological, social, and moral superstitions. Atoms are like citizens of the natural kingdom, of which God is the legislator, policeman, and judge. Even today, it is common for scientists to say that they are studying not nature but the mind of God, whose laws are written in mathematical language.

Nietzsche regards such blatant anthropomorphism as ridiculous. God is an anthropomorphic projection, and the notion of natural law is no more than the projection of human social and moral conventions into non-human nature. Nature neither obeys laws; in nature "there are only necessities: there is nobody who commands, nobody who obeys, nobody who trespasses" (GS 109).

Scientific theories are saturated with human political values. Atomic materialism is a world-view that corresponds to modern democratic political values. Just as a democratic society is a plurality of human units all politically equal under the law, so too all materialistic atoms are mechanistically equal under the laws of nature. (BGE 22). We ought to recognize that such science is interpretation of the world from a human, all-too human perspective.

Nietzsche rejects Newtonian mechanistic science. The world is not a machine: "it is certainly not constructed for one purpose, and calling it a "machine" does it far too much honor." (GS 109) Theists use the notion that the world is a machine to argue for their theory of God like this: the world is a machine; every machine has a designer; so the world has a designer, namely, God. The error, of course, is that theists confuse order (which is merely mathematical) with design.

Nietzsche's skeptical philosophy of science shows how mechanistic science is derived from our psychology: "All the presuppositions of mechanistic theory -- matter, atom, gravity, pressure and stress -- are not 'facts-in-themselves' but interpretations with the aid of psychical fictions." (WTP 689) For example, "Gravity itself has no mechanistic cause, since it itself is the ground of mechanistic results" (WP 689); so gravity has to have some other origin -- the will. The problem is not that gravity is a psychical fiction; rather, the problem is that it is linked to nihilistic Christian theology. Newton thought of space-time as "God's sensorium" (as God's consciousness); so the universal force is God's will. But that is nihilistic (WP 707, 708).

Science, no matter how advanced, no matter how highly formalized by abstract mathematics, is at most only an "attempt to humanize things as faithfully as possible; as we describe things and their one-after-another, we learn how to describe ourselves more and more precisely" (GS 112). Since Nietzsche argues that any cognition that leads to truth is essentially limited by its original biological utility, he does not think it is possible (or even desirable) for science to aim at some impersonal objectivity. Scientific thought necessarily remains anthropocentric. The best that is possible is for science to become self-consciously aware of its humanizations of nature, so that it is able to project into nature those human social values that are most life-affirming and world-affirming. While it is necessary for science to project human moral fictions into nature, it is not necessary for it to project nihilistic moral fictions into nature. It is possible for science to become self-conscious and affirmative.

10. Mathematics

Nietzsche's attitude towards mathematics is quite positive. He thinks mathematics is the means to ultimate human self-knowledge:

> Let us introduce the refinement and rigor of mathematics into all sciences as far as this is at all possible, not in the faith that this will lead us to know things but in order to *determine* our human relation to things. Mathematics is merely the means for general and ultimate knowledge of man. (GS 246)

Since Nietzsche thinks that self-knowledge is basically the awareness of how thought deceives itself for the sake of life, it should come as no surprise that Nietzsche admires mathematics precisely because its concepts emerge from the root of the self-interpretation of thought. Mathematics is the deepest artistry of the mind.

Errors involving identity and equality (that there are self-identical or equal things) are the most basic of all biologically useful errors; they are the errors that are most necessary for life; and since mathematics is the science of identity and equality as such, it is the science of the original and most biologically useful errors:

> The laws of numbers were invented on the basis of the initially prevailing error that there are various identical things (but actually there is nothing identical) or at least that there are things (but there is no "thing"). The assumption of multiplicity always presumes that there is something, which occurs repeatedly. But this is just where error rules; even here, we invent entities, unities, that do not exist. . . . To a world that is *not* our idea, the laws of numbers are completely inapplicable: they are valid only in the human world. (HH I:19)

To think mathematically is to think consciously in a way that the most primitive forms of life think unconsciously. The original living things are the first things in the universe that are self-reproducing; they are the original recurrent identical cases. Mathematical thought reaches all the way down to very origin of life in the inorganic.

Mathematics is the science of pure self-deception. The study of the mathematical world of purely formal abstract objects reveals to the conscious mind the deepest mechanisms of unconscious mental life. Self-knowledge requires knowledge of these mechanisms: that's why mathematics is the means to ultimate human self-knowledge.

In modern Western cultures, it is fashionable to oppose mathematics to art. If Nietzsche is right, then that opposition is wrong.

34

According to Nietzsche, mathematics studies the most artistic and imaginative powers of human life. Mathematics studies the form-giving powers, which imaginatively project structure into the chaos of events. The mathematical imagination is the most artistic of all.[2]

Importantly, Nietzsche argues that mathematical thought is the most dangerous kind of thought precisely because it reveals the conditions of existence that make thought itself possible in the universe. When it thinks mathematically, thought thinks at its very limit. That limit is dangerous because it is precisely when thought thinks of the origin of its existence that it is most tempted to think of its existence as if it were an origin: in doing mathematics, thought risks the greatest self-deception, for it risks thinking that it is the origin of existence rather than thinking that existence is the origin of it.

The greatest danger for thought is for ascetic supernaturalism to use mathematical thinking to justify its otherworldliness. When it does mathematics, consciousness has access to the cognitive operations of equalization and identity; so when it ascribes values to the system of abstract objects revealed by mathematics, consciousness is ascribing values to the deepest and most vital operations of cognition (which have the greatest biological utility and so are the most necessary for human survival); if ascetic supernaturalism corrupts mathematics, it has corrupted all cognition. When mathematics is rendered nihilistic, thought itself is rendered nihilistic. Unfortunately, Nietzsche thinks that this is exactly what has happened. Platonism is the corruption of mathematical thought by nihilistic values. The supernatural world (the real and true world) is the world of abstract mathematical objects.

The transvaluation of values, the conversion of nihilistic negation into Dionysian affirmation, has to begin with a transvaluation of the meaning of mathematical thinking. Mathematics does not reveal the true world. Mathematics does not give us access to any God's-Eye View. Mathematics must be reconceptualized as Dionysian art. As it becomes conscious of itself as an aesthetic process, it is able to become life- and world-affirming. *Dionysian mathematics* is mathematics in the grand style (WP 800, 842). Dionysian mathematics avoids the nihilistic self-deception that formal objects (points, lines, planes, numbers) really exist in some true other world; instead, it affirms that our deepest articles of faith (that there are self-identical things, that things fall into classes) are true just because they have the greatest biological utility -- the greatest *power*. Dionysian mathematics harnesses the will to truth to the will to life. Instead of suppressing the vital power of existence at its origin, it intensifies that vitality.[3]

11. The Virtuous Circle of Knowledge

So far Nietzsche's entire argument about knowledge presupposes that his evolutionary assumptions are true. To be consistent, he isn't able to exclude those presuppositions from his arguments about truth and knowledge. Since our knowledge includes the evolutionary theory of truth, it is applicable to itself, so it must be applied to itself.

Some theories of knowledge refute themselves when they are applied to themselves. The most famous example of self-refutation is the positivistic theory of knowledge. Positivism says that propositions are either meaningless or meaningful; only meaningful propositions are true or false; meaningless propositions are nonsense. It defines meaningfulness like this: "The meaning of a proposition is the set of possible experiences that it implies." Since that proposition does not imply any possible experiences, it is meaningless. So it is nonsense. It is self-refuting or self-confounding. It defeats itself.

The evolutionary theory of truth says that all knowledge is no more than a system of propositions consistent with those articles of faith without which human animals are not able to survive. Therefore, if we assume it is true, and if we apply it to itself, it then tells us that the evolutionary theory of truth is at most a system of propositions consistent with those articles of faith without which human animals are not able to survive -- and that does not refute itself.

Of course, if it is true that the only perspectives that evolve are the ones that facilitate for their own evolution, this very account of the evolution of perspectives applies to itself, and it tells us that it is true because (and only because) it facilitates its own evolution. And since it is a theory that has evolved, it has justified itself. Applied to itself, it is self-justifying. Now we are cycling in another Nietzschean circle. We are staring into another Nietzschean mirror that reflects only itself reflecting itself reflecting itself . . . But the circle is not vicious, and the mirroring is not vacuous. The mirroring is self--affirming.

The self-justification of the evolutionary theory of knowledge is like the self-justification of the theory of inductive knowledge. Inductive knowledge is general knowledge inferred from special cases. You see that the sun has always risen; so you conclude it will rise tomorrow. But the fact that it has risen in the past does not logically imply that it will rise in the future, unless you add another principle -- one that lets you reach a general conclusion ("The sun always rises" or "The future is always like the past") on the basis of specific facts ("The sun rose today"). There is no logical way to reach any general conclusion from specific facts unless induction is true; but the only evidence you can have for induction (if you're not omniscient) is based on specific facts. Fortunately, induction does not negate itself when it is applied to itself; rather, it affirms itself. Each time the sun actually rises, you have both more evidence for the general conclusion that it will rise in the future, as well as more evidence for the theory that induction leads to true knowledge. Induction justifies induction. It is self-affirming, like Nietzsche's evolutionary theory.

12. The Joyful Wisdom

Nietzsche is acutely aware of all the circles (virtuous and vicious) in the theory of knowledge. Ascetic supernaturalists often say that life on earth is (false) like a dream; life in the spirit-world or soul-world is (true) like wakefulness. The wakefulness that Nietzsche advises is a sort of lucid dreaming inside the perspectival system. We are not able to escape from the perspectival rule that any perspective on the universe is from within the universe, and so must be consistent with itself when applied to itself . Nietzsche says: "I suddenly woke up in the midst of this dream, but only to the consciousness that I am dreaming that I must go on dreaming lest I perish" (GS 54).

Ascetic supernaturalism asserts that there is some "God's-Eye View" on the universe from outside of the universe, and that all knowledge from that viewpoint is absolutely true. Ascetic supernaturalism does not respect the practical (i.e. pragmatic) limit that utility places on perspectival truth, since it denies that truth is perspectival. Since ascetic supernaturalism says that humans are not animals (they are unnatural souls), it does not consider the survival value of a proposition (especially moral laws) when it declares them to be eternally or absolutely true. Morality is not justified by its biological utility for the human species, but by its consistency with "God's will" or "God's law". Ascetic supernaturalism has a will to truth that exceeds the limits of biological utility (GS 110). That will to truth is a will to death (GS 344). Its will to truth is nihilistic.

Nietzsche opposes that nihilistic will to truth with the aesthetic self-consistency of his joyful wisdom (GS 113; AOM 180). The joyful wisdom integrates all the imaginative and critical faculties of human animals to optimize the vitality of human animals, to help us flourish and thrive. Indeed, the joyful wisdom aims to so intensely enhance the vitality of the human species that it becomes superhuman, that it lives with that intensity than which none greater is possible:

men are capable of consciously resolving to evolve themselves to a new culture, whereas formerly they did so unconsciously and fortuitously: they can now create better conditions for the propagation of men and for their nutrition, education and instruction, manage the earth as a whole economically, balance and employ the powers of men in general. This new, conscious culture destroys the old, which viewed as a whole has led an unconscious animal- and plant-life (HH I:24, I:25)

The most profound theory of truth that is possible within an evolved perspective is that life is like a dream and that the role of truth for life is the enhancement and extension of that dream. It is the realization

> that among all these dreamers, I, too, who "know" am dancing my dance; that the knower is a means for prolonging the earthly dance and thus belongs to the masters of the ceremony of existence; and that the sublime consistency and interrelatedness of all knowledge perhaps is and will be the highest means to *preserve* the universality of dreaming and the mutual comprehension of all dreamers and also *the continuation of the dream.* (GS 54)

13. Self-Conscious Science

Because we are in the universe, all our scientific descriptions of the universe necessarily contain descriptions of our own selves engaged in the activity of description. We cannot avoid projecting our self-interpretations into our scientific theories, since the very appearance of natural phenomena (empirical facts) presupposes interpretation by the human mind. Since it is logically necessary that we theorize about the universe from some perspective inside the universe, and since it is logically necessary that every perspective on the universe is self-including and self-reflecting, every theory of the universe (no matter how scientific or objective) presupposes a theory of the self. It is a pure logical fact that our theories include our self-conceptions. The universe is like a mirror: as we look into it, we project our self-conceptions into it, and our truest scientific theories are reflections of our self-conceptions. Any scientific theory that aims at truth has to incorporate this self-mirroring in a some way (BGE 24).

Supposing that instead of denying that our knowledge is made in our own image, we recognize that all knowledge includes self-knowledge, that it includes the structure of the knower: "Suppose nothing else were 'given' as real except our world of desires and passions, and we could not get down, or up, to any other 'reality' besides the reality of our drives -- for thinking is merely a relation of these drives to each other" (BGE 36). Suppose we recognize that this fact about the given is "sufficient for also understanding . . . the so-called mechanistic (or "material") world" (BGE 36). In recognizing this, we do not become subjective idealists like Berkeley or Schopenhauer (BGE 36); rather, we are affirming that in order to for our knowledge of the world to become objective, our knowledge of our selves must become equally objective. No objective knowledge of the world without objective knowledge of the self. That's the price for knowledge, since every internal perspective on the universe includes a perspective on itself, and must be reflexively self-consistent.

The physical universe has the same "rank of reality as our affect"; it is a "more primitive form of the world of affects in which everything still lies contained in a powerful unity" (BGE 36). Since we can't help but think of causality in terms of our own willing, the scientific method has to be augmented with a self-conscious recognition of this fact: we must not assume any other kind of causality until we have pushed the idea that all causality is willing to its logical extreme:

> [if] we really recognize the will as efficient, [if] we believe in the causality of the will: if we do -- and at bottom our faith in this is nothing less than our faith in causality itself -- then we have to make the experiment of positing the causality of the will hypothetically as the only one. 'Will,' of course, can affect only 'will' -- and not 'matter' . . . one has to risk the hypothesis whether will does not affect will wherever 'effects' are recognized -- and whether all mechanical occurrences are not, insofar as force is active in them, will force, effects of will. (BGE 36)

For Nietzsche, all will is will to power -- the will to actualize all the possibilities of the willing agency. So self-conscious science, insofar as it recognizes that all knowledge presupposes self-knowledge, must recognize that all mechanical force is will to power if it utilizes the concept of force at all. Any science that uses causality presupposes the will, and so presupposes the will to power, and has to recognize that presupposition in order to be objective.

Nietzsche's theory that the world is will to power and nothing else (BGE 36; WP 1067) is based on his epistemological argument that all knowledge is self-knowledge, since all logically possible perspectives on the world are perspectives from within the world. The will to power as an objective hypothesis about existence (an ontological hypothesis) emerges from his epistemology.

Although we can't avoid projecting the self and will into our scientific theories, we can avoid projecting nihilistic interpretations of the self and will -- we can avoid projecting nihilistic values into our theories. We necessarily project our self-evaluations into our science, but we are free to determine the self-evaluation we project. So, instead of projecting Platonic-Christian values into our science, Nietzsche wants to project affirmative values. We can have an affirmative science (a joyful wisdom) once we have affirmative conceptions of the self and the will. We need new conceptions of self and will.

14. Reconceiving the Self and the Will

Nietzsche rejects the notion that there is a unified "I" or integrated ego behind the "I think" (BGE 17). The self is not a solid being; it is not a static unity but rather a dynamic multiplicity. There is no one active homunculus in the mind manipulating passive ideas or directing psychic processes. He objects to the belief that in soul as something "indestructible, eternal, indivisible, as a monad, as an *atomon*" (BGE 12). He opposes the notion that the ego or soul is a permanent unity. The self is not an eternally enduring substance. The self is not any single being; it is a multiplicity of becomings (WP 492).

The repudiation of the immortal and unitary soul does not do away with the idea of the soul altogether. On the contrary, the ego or soul remains a useful and fruitful hypothesis for psychology, and thus for physics. The way is cleared for new theories of the soul, such as "mortal soul," and "soul as subjective multiplicity," and "soul as social structure of the drives and affects" (BGE 12).

The mind is unified, but for Nietzsche "All unity is unity only as organization and co-operation" (WTP 561). The mind is like a city whose citizens are ideas (concepts, images, sensations, etc.). Ideas are active: every idea has a life of its own; it comes when it will (BGE 17). Thinking emerges from the interactions of ideas.

Nietzsche's theory of mind has a distinctively social and hierarchical flavor.[4] Nietzsche tells us that the body is "but a social structure composed of many souls." (BGE 19). These visceral souls are the instinctual impulses of the body at the cellular level. For Nietzsche rejects the Cartesian distinction between mind and body: mind emerges from the self-organization of bodily energies. The souls that make up the body organize themselves into a hierarchical social or political structure in which some rule and others are ruled (BGE 19). Thinking is a result of this social organization of instinctual drives, for it is "merely a relation of these drives to each other" (BGE 36). In other words, conscious thinking "is actually nothing but a *certain behavior of the instincts toward one another*" (GS 333).

Just as the self needs to be thought of differently, so also the will needs to be thought of differently. Nietzsche believes the will is complex. The will is not one force, but many coordinated impulses: it is the emergence of a harmony among the drives of the ideas (BGE 19).

Will emerges from the dynamical social coordination of many "under-wills" or "under-souls" (BGE 19). Will is concerted effort.

The will, for Nietzsche, does not proceed from an initial state to any goal state envisioned in advance. The will has motives, but its only objective is immediate self-enhancement. The will improves itself here and now. It optimizes itself in its local context. The will has no long-distance goal. There is no *purpose* in the will. Rather, one will ends where it is stopped by another will, but it interprets that stop as if the stop were its objective, as if the stop were a goal.

So there is no will at all in the sense of a goal-directed or purpo-sive force; rather, there is will only as the negotiated agreements (actions and reactions). There are only *treaty-drafts of will* (WP 715), which are ephemeral and infinitesimal discharges of will. Every endur-ing unit is some self-reproducing or self-repeating organization of these treaty-drafts of will, these instantaneous flashes of mortal souls.

Self-knowledge freed from the Platonic-Christian conceptions of the self and the will (conceptions which were based on nihilistic values) recognizes that the self and the will are multiplicities of events that oc-cur (that flash like bolts of lightning) and that organize themselves into self-reproducing arrangements by means of their attractions and repul-sions. Every physical thing, including the whole physical universe, is a self-repeating complex of events in the world.

Endnotes.

1. Nietzsche defines identity in terms of recurrence (WP 512, 521, 532, 544, 551, 552, 568, 569). This principle applies to every whole space-time physical universe.
2. Nietzsche's philosophy of mathematics is echoed in many respects by the modern mathematicians known as intuitionists. It also has many affinities with the structuralist approach to mathematics.
3. The basic objects of modern mathematics are sets. The universe of sets shares these features with Nietzsche's world as will to power: it is purely relational; every set is a unique individual; all relations of sets are necessary; the universe of sets is excessive insofar as set-theory always strives for more levels; all form in the universe of sets is recurrent, in the sense that every theory has many models.
4. Nietzsche is not the first to propose a social model of mind. Plato says the soul is a city (*Republic*, 435c-441). Again, Nietzsche's social model of mind recalls and re-interprets Plato's model. Compare Nietzsche's use of the notion of aristocracy in WP 490 with Plato's notion of aristocracy in Book VIII of the *Republic*.

4
The Will to Power

1. The Continuous Flux of Possibilities

Nietzsche is deeply influenced by the ancient Greek thinker *Heraclitus*. Heraclitus is famous for saying "You can never step into the same river twice." He thought that everything is always changing, so that there are no enduring things that stay the same. Permanence and persistence are illusions. Things *look* the same, but in reality they are always differing from what they were. Because the flames in a fire do not stay the same, but flash continuously into other forms, Heraclitus said the universe is like fire. There are no things, just flashes.

The solidity and stability of things like rocks, tables, and even our own bodies, is a trick of our senses. Science tells us that the rock is made of atoms whose parts are always moving. The parts of atoms are particles like electrons, protons, and neutrons. But these parts are not stable things; they aren't like little eternal rocks: they are more like waves in an ocean of energy. Perhaps that energy is like the Heraclitean fire, so that particles are like flames flickering in and out of actuality. If that's right, our universe is just a kind of self-ordering of these flashes.

Nietzsche updates Heraclitus. He doesn't think the universe is literally made of fire. He updates the Heraclitean fire by interpreting it as *force*. Nietzsche says there are no unchanging beings; rather, there are only becomings: "Continual transition forbids us to speak of 'individuals,' etc.; the 'number' of beings is itself in flux" (WP 520).

Nietzsche thinks that the flux is continuous. It never makes jumps or leaps from one arrangement to another; rather, it flows smoothly like liquid fire. The flux is continuous in the sense that if you isolate or separate any two parts of the flux (say, here and there, or now and then),

42

there are still other parts of the flux in between the parts that you isolated. You can never wholly divide the flux, you can't chop or cut it in half, because there's always going to be some undivided flux in the cut that joins the parts you tried to separate. The flux is like a smooth and indivisible ocean, a seamless whole. It is "a continuous, homogeneous, undivided, indivisible flowing" (WS 11; GS 111). There is no cause and effect in the flux; there are no beings to act as causes. There are just flows of force. When we say *this* is the cause and *that* is the effect, we erroneously divide the flux into two isolated pieces between which we think there is nothing. But between cause and effect there are infinitely many processes we do not see (GS 112).

While Nietzsche gets the idea of flux from Heraclitus, he gets the idea of continuity, of smoothness or gaplessness, from the 17th century German thinker Leibniz.[1] Leibniz thinks the universe is continuous. He thinks the physical universe is produced by the interactions of tiny particles he calls monads. Monads are like geometrical points. They are infinitely small (infinitesimal) in space. Space is filled with monads. Space is packed so tight with monads that between any two monads there is another one, just like between any two points on a line there is another point. There are no gaps between monads. No monads are missing from the universe: anywhere a monad could be, there some monad actually is. The collection of monads is a totality without any gaps. A full totality is called a *plenum* (as in "plenty").

Leibniz also has some Heraclitean ideas: every monad is like a tiny Heraclitean river. There's time-flow going on in the monad, although the monad itself does not change. Monads persist: they are enduring things that keep their identities over time. Nevertheless, the internal details of the monads change, and they change continuously. Time burns inside the monad; they are little balls of Heraclitean fire.

2. There are no Equal Things

Since reality is ultimately continuous flux, there are no things that are equal to themselves for any longer than an instant: there are no persistent or enduring things. No thing is self-identical for any duration in time or change in space. So X=X is true only at a point-instant, only here and now, because X is not a being, but a becoming, an event, a flash of fire, a lightning-strike. There are no things, there are only events that are *point-instants of force:* this force right here right now. No two point-instants of force are identical (WS 11; GS 110, 111).

There is only one instance of every individual in the universe; there are not many instances of one thing: "The assumption of plurality always presupposes the existence of something that occurs more than once: but precisely here error already holds sway." (HH I:19) So there are never multiple occurrences of the same thing.

Every physical thing is unique and has exactly one occurrence in the universe: "it is certain that one leaf is never totally the same as another" (PT, p. 83) In particular, our lives are unique parts of the universe and do not occur multiply: "In his heart every man knows quite well that, being unique, he will be in the world only once and that no imaginable chance will for a second time gather together into a unity so strangely variegated an assortment like he is" (UM 3, p. 127); "all our actions are altogether incomparably personal, unique, and infinitely individual" (GS 354; HH I:286)

Nietzsche reasons correctly when he says that pure becoming implies that there is no invariance of identity through change in space and time. But the idea that there are no equal things is not original with him. Once again, this is a Leibnizian idea. Leibniz says that no two monads are every the same, they all differ. Still, Leibniz didn't take his theory of monads far enough. Monads are minimally extended in space, but maximally extended in time. Leibniz should have said that the monads are infinitesimal spatially and infinitesimal temporally.

Nietzsche takes Leibniz's notion of monads to its logical extreme by recapturing its Heraclitean spirit. He says: "We may venture to speak of atoms and monads in a relative sense" (WP 715), and these are not enduring things, but events. While Leibniz's monads are like little balls of fire that flicker, Nietzsche's events are just flashes of flame. Nietzsche's events are minimally extended in space and time.[2]

Events are packed tightly together in a plenum; no point-instant of force is missing from the world (WP 1067). If you compare any two events, however similar, there is some other event in between them that is more similar to each of them. Every possible combination of events is in the world.[3] For Nietzsche, the physical part of the world (nature) is the collection of all possible combinations of point-instants of force. Every physical universe is a possible organization of nature; there are many possible organizations of nature.

3. The World of Relationships

One of the most powerful facts about relations is that the relations can remain the same while the things involved in those relations change. For instance, suppose you are playing a game of checkers; you and your partner start with all the usual red and black wooden disks in the standard initial configuration on a checker board; you and your partner make one move after another according to the usual rules, except that after each move you replace your pieces with pennies and your partner replaces his or her pieces with quarters. The game goes on as usual; it doesn't matter that the things are changing so long as the relations between them stay the same.

Since events are not extended in space and time, any physical things that are extended in space and time are structures or arrangements of events. All material things are *complexes* of events. This is true for the smallest things, like subatomic particles, to the largest things, like the universe. Ultimately, the world is a system of relations:

> the world, apart from our condition of living in it, the world that we have not reduced to our being, our logic and psychological prejudices, does not exist as a world 'in-itself'; it is essentially a world of relationships; . . . its being is essentially different from every point; it presses upon every point, every point resists it -- and the sum of these [pressures and resistances] is in every case quite incongruent. (WP 568).

No two events are the same. So if there is any identity or unity in existence, it occurs only among complexes of events (WP 552c, 561). Events are never the same, although arrangements and structures of events are sometimes the same. The parts of any physical whole are never the same at different places or times; but since every whole is an arrangement of parts, the whole can be the same even though its parts differ. Physical wholes (from atoms to bodies to universes) are complexes of events that vary both in space and in time. Since it is possible to preserve the relations among events while the events change in space and time, it is possible to preserve the structure of the complex and therefore to have a thing that seems to be extended in space and time. We forget that physical wholes are arrangements; we think (erroneously) that they are substantial units.

Natural science is a theory only of relations: "All laws of nature are only relations between x, y, and z. We define laws of nature as relations to an x, y, and z -- each of which we are in turn acquainted with only in relation to other x, y, and z's." (PT, p. 51); "what is a law of nature as such for us? We are not acquainted with it in itself, but only with its effects, which means in its relation to other laws of nature -- which, in turn, are known to us only as sums of relations" (PT, p. 87). So the physical universe is a system of relations among events, a network of interconnected point-instants of force.

4. Striving for Power over Everything

Nietzsche says that the world is will to power and nothing besides (WP 1067). To figure out what this means, suppose we start with the theory that the will to power is some tyrannical egotistical desire that people have to dominate or master other people. If that striving has an explanation, it is not basic and so is just an expression of the will to power and not the will to power itself.

The political theory that people strive for power over other people does not originate with Nietzsche. It's as old as history itself. But to focus our ideas, we can pick one philosopher who developed the idea clearly: the 17th century British thinker Thomas Hobbes. Hobbes argues that politically organized human communities evolve out of a state of nature in which there is a violent struggle for existence that is a war of all against all. Underneath this political striving there is a deeper biological striving: human animals want to live, to reproduce. But biological life and reproduction requires resources, and resources are scarce; so people struggle with one another for scarce resources.

So political striving is an expression of the will to power, not the will to power itself. The will to power appears, on a deeper level, to be a biological striving. All political competition for scarce resources and security serves the deeper purpose of biological reproduction. But if this biological striving has an explanation, then it too is not basic and so is an expression of the will to power rather than the will to power itself. To analyze biological striving we need to turn from Hobbes to Darwin. Darwin's theory of evolution by natural selection had a deep impact on Nietzsche. Darwin was influenced by Hobbes.

In *The Origin of Species*, Darwin applies the Hobbesian idea of the state of nature as a war of all against all to the whole universe of living and reproducing organisms:

> each organic being is striving to increase at a geometrical ratio; that each at some period of its life, during some season of the year, during each generation or at intervals, has to struggle for life and to suffer great destruction. When we reflect on this struggle, we may console ourselves with the full belief, that the war of nature is not incessant, that no fear is felt, that death is generally prompt, and that the vigorous, the healthy, and the happy survive and multiply. (Darwin, p. 129)[4]

The biological struggle for existence is not basic. It is an effect of the *excessive* rate of reproduction of organisms: "A struggle for existence inevitably follows from the high rate at which all organic beings tend to increase." (Darwin, p. 116) The high rate of reproduction is what makes all resources scarce eventually, so that competition occurs.

It is often said that Darwin thinks life is purposeless. That is wrong. Every living thing has a primary purpose or goal for which it strives: "every single organic being around us may be said to be striving to the utmost to increase in numbers" (Darwin, p. 119, 157). When Darwin speaks of striving or trying, he almost always talks about it in this mathematical sense, as a striving to increase numerically.

Every organism strives to maximize the number of its offspring, to make more instances of its own species or type. This *striving for power over number* is far deeper than any striving for mastery over scarce resources or other organisms. It is the deepest striving, which has no biological explanation. The striving to increase numerically is the will to power in life.

So biological striving is an expression of the will to power, not the will to power itself. The will to power appears, on a deeper level, to be this mathematical striving for victory over number. Now this is a truly odd kind of striving: how is it possible to strive for victory over number? This quantitative striving is the striving to be greater, to be more, to exceed, to surpass every limit. The striving for victory over number is the will to be beyond any limitation.

5. Logical Striving for Victory over Limitation

The mathematical striving for victory over number is really a kind of logical striving for victory over limitation. The series of transitions from 0 to 1, from 1 to 2, and from 2 to ∞ is the victory of something over nothing, of many over one, of the infinite over the finite. The striving for victory over limitation explains why there is something rather than nothing: something is greater than nothing.

It is hard to see how there could be any striving more basic than the striving for victory over limitation, since that striving is so abstract it lies at the root of all other striving. The striving to surpass limitation is the most general kind of striving, since it is the striving to exceed any restriction, to not be constrained in any way.

The will to power is ultimately the striving to exceed limitation in its most abstract logical sense. But if the will to power is the will to be beyond every limitation in the most extreme sense, then power itself is just being greater than every limit; power itself is that than which no greater is possible. Power is not power over this or that fact, it is power over all possible facts -- it power over possibility itself. It is the power to make every possibility actual. It is hard to see how any power could be more powerful than the power to make all possible beings actually be. The will to power is the striving to be power, the striving to be that power than which no greater is possible. The will to power aims at omnipotence, at absolutely infinite power, which is the power to make every possible being actually exist.

Absolute power (omnipotence), exceeding all limits, and being that than which no greater is possible, are all traditional attributes of God. But the God of which they are attributes isn't quite the Christian God, the moral God of the New Testament. The idea of God as sheer power is more of an Old Testament notion. At one point Nietzsche says: "Let us remove supreme goodness from the concept of God: it is unworthy of a god. Let us also remove supreme wisdom . . . God the *supreme power* -- that suffices! Everything follows from it, 'the world' follows from it!" (WP 1037). Still, Nietzsche doesn't really think that God is power; it's more accurate to say he thinks that *power is divine*.

6. The Striving Possibles

We've already seen how many aspects of Nietzsche's thought are inspired by Leibniz. The will to power is no exception. Leibniz says that possibilities strive to be actual.[5] For instance, an oak tree that is the possibility of an acorn strives to be actual and therefore causes the acorn to develop. The striving is done by the possible oak tree and not by the actual acorn. Possibilities strive.

Leibniz says that all possible things strive to be actual; this struggle for actual existence is like the Darwinian struggle for life in the sense that actuality is a scarce resource for which all possible things have to compete. They have to compete for actuality because, according to Leibniz, many possibilities are logically opposed to one another, and they cannot both be actual. If you toss a coin, it is possible that it lands heads up or tails up, but not both. Each of these possibilities excludes the other. Both cannot be actual in the same universe.

Not all possibilities *exclude* all other possibilities. Some possibilities *include* other possibilities. The possibilities that cooperate with one another form groups that strive for actuality together, so that their *collective striving* is greater than their separate striving.

All possibilities both compete against and cooperate with one another for actuality. All possibilities interact logically (not physically) with one another, logically affirming or logically negating one another's claims to actuality. Leibniz asserts that:

> *Everything possible demands that it should exist*, and hence will exist unless something else prevents it, which also demands that it

should exist and is incompatible with the former; and hence it follows that the combination of things always exists by which the greatest possible number of things exists; as, if we assume A, B, C, D, to be equal as regards essence, i.e. equally perfect, or equally demanding existence, and if we assume that D is incompatible with A and with B, while A is compatible with any except D, and similarly as regards B and C; it follows that the combination ABC, excluding D, will exist; for if we wish D to exi.t, it can only coexist with C, and hence the combination CD will exist, which is more imperfect than the combination ABC.[6]

When Leibniz says that "the combination of things always exists by which the greatest possible number of things exists", you can see the numerical version of the will to power at work.

Leibniz says that perfection of any combination of possibilities is the measure of its striving for actuality. Perfection is activity. A thing "is said *to act* externally insofar as it has perfection, and *to react* to another insofar as it is imperfect." (M 49) Here you see Nietzsche's own doctrine of *activity and reactivity* in a nutshell.

Nietzsche only partly agrees with Leibniz. Leibniz says that the striving possibilities have to ask God for actuality; perfection is the measure of God's willingness to bestow actuality. The possibilities compete and cooperate in the mind of God prior to the creation of the actual universe. Leibniz says "as soon as God has decreed to create something there is a struggle between all the possibles, all of them laying claim to existence, and that those which, being united, produce most reality, most perfection, most significance carry the day."[7] God judges all the possibilities. Only a select few, approved by God, get to be actual. The power of God is limited by God's morality. Nietzsche objects to this moral constraint on the actualization of possibilities.

7. That No Than Which No Greater is Possible

If you toss a coin, it is possible that it lands heads up or tails up, but not both. Each of these possibilities excludes the other. Both cannot be actual in one universe. But what if this is not the only universe? There may be a different universe for each different possibility. In one universe the coin comes up heads, in another it comes up tails.

There's nothing *logically* wrong with the theory that there are many possible physical universes. The alternative is that no other universe is even *possible*, which means that any other universe is impossible. If our universe is the only possible universe, then the nature of our universe is necessary. The natural laws of our universe (for instance, e = mc^2) are logically necessary. To say that something is logically necessary means that anything else leads to a contradiction. But it's hard to see why e = mc^3 leads to a *contradiction*. It leads to a very different universe, but there's nothing *logically* wrong with that. Leibniz is the first to seriously develop the idea that there are many possible universes. Any statement that is not self-contradictory is true of some possible universe. For instance: "I have three heads" is true of all those universes in which I do have three heads. But that is not actually the case. I actually have only one head. Leibniz says that while there are many possible universes, just one is actual. This is where Nietzsche's will to power differs from Leibniz's striving. For Nietzsche, the will to power actualizes all possible combinations of events, and so actualizes all physically possible universes.^{8}

Leibniz argues for an extremely restricted affirmation: from the totality of possible combinations of events, God actualizes only one. Actuality is denied to all other possible universes. Leibniz says that the universe God selects for actualization is the best of all possible universes: while this universe has some evil, every other possible universe has even more evil. So God is not really responsible for the evil that exists in the universe. No other possible universe is better than this one. It doesn't get any better than this. It's a joke that goes like this: the optimist says this is the best of all possible universes; the pessimist agrees. But it was either this universe or none at all, and the worst situation is no universe at all. So, here we are, in this world, on this earth, with these bodies.

The argument that God selected the best of all possible universes for actualization is intended to reconcile God's omnipotence and goodness with the existence of actual evil. Leibniz is fighting hard against an old argument for the non-existence of the Christian God. It goes like this: God is good and all-powerful; a good being does not want evil to exist and does not want to permit evil to exist; an all-powerful being does whatever it wants and does not permit whatever it does not want; but, there is evil; so, either God is not good or God is not all-powerful; but it was said that God is both good and all-powerful; so, (the Christian) God does not exist. Leibniz fights this argument with a counter-argument, the argument that this is the best of all possible universes. Any argument that tries to explain why a good and all-powerful God created a universe with evil in it is called a *theodicy*. Nietzsche accuses Leibniz of practicing *negative theodicy* (WP 411, 419; BGE 207; GS 370). Leibniz's God negates most strivings.

For Leibniz, all possibles strive for actuality; but the actuality toward which they strive is the old Christian-Platonic God. So their striving (their will to power) meets an objection, a divine "No!" in the form of God's moral evaluation. God judges the universes and finds all but one unworthy of actuality. God denies actuality to all universes but one. This denial is the supreme No! It is that No! than which none is greater. The Christian-Platonic God is extreme negativity.

In contrast, Nietzsche wants a theodicy that is absolutely affirmative. Nietzsche's affirmative theodicy won't affirm the reality of anything like the Christian God. No God is needed. It will affirm the divinity of the striving possibles themselves, by granting them *all* actuality. It is that Yes! than which there is no greater.

8. The Dice Game

Of all the ideas Nietzsche takes from Heraclitus, the one that most deeply influenced him is the idea of *the dice game*. From the early writings in1874 to the end in 1888, the dice game is a central image. I know of no other concept or image that recurs so frequently over the entire course of Nietzsche's philosophical career.

Heraclitus says that existence is a kind of dice game played by an innocent god, a god who is a child. Nietzsche approves of Heraclitus's assertion that "The world is a game Zeus plays", or, even better, that the world is the game "of the fire with itself." Strikingly, Nietzsche adds that "this is the only sense in which the one is at the same time the many." (PTG 6, p. 58; PTG 14, p. 91)   Humanity is an exceptional throw "in the game of dice played by Heraclitus' great 'child' be he called Zeus or chance" (GM 2:16). Human politics is a dice game (GS 40). The superhuman is a lucky roll (GS 288).

Zarathustra proclaims that existence is a divine dice game: "Above all things stands the heaven of chance, the heaven of innocence, the heaven of accident"; (Z 3:4). Zarathustra says of this heaven of chance that "you are to me a dance floor for divine chances, that you are to me a gods' table for divine dice and dicers!" (Z 3:4)

In the dice game, the faces of the die are the possibilities; the side of the die that lands up on the dice-table is actualized. The dice game is Nietzsche's version of striving possibles. Instead of ending with that No! than which none is greater, Nietzsche's version of the striving possibles ends with that Yes! than which none is greater.

He says the dice game is played by time (the Aeon) and it is played without any wisdom: "the endless stupid game which the great child, time, plays before us and with us" (UM 3, p. 155). The dice game frees the striving possibilities from any selection based on the will or morality of a wise God: "'Lord Chance' -- he is the world's oldest nobility, which I have given back to all things; I have released them from servitude under purpose. . . . no 'eternal will' acts over them and through them" (Z 3:4; D 13). When the die is thrown, no single outcome is selected as the basis for all further throws; rather, every outcome is selected as the basis for all further throws.

The dice game is an infinite game that necessarily actualizes even those combinations of events that least resemble chance: "Those iron hands of necessity which shake the dice-box of chance play their game for an infinite length of time: so that there *have* to be throws which exactly resemble purposiveness and rationality of every degree" (D 130). Nietzsche says that even the luckiest throws have to occur, because in an infinite time all throws have to occur. But if the die is truly thrown randomly, that is false. The sequence of coin tosses that is always heads is a random sequence. The idea that every combination of throws *necessarily* occurs is far stronger than randomness. The dice game is the logical principle that every possibility necessarily occurs. The Heraclitean child is the will to power as absolute affirmation: it throws every possible sequence

Every throw of the die produces something novel and unique, in the sense that it extends the whole past existing chain of throws in new ways. Nietzsche says "the dice-game of chance and the future could never again produce anything exactly similar to what it produced in the past" (UM 2, p. 70). The only explanation for this is that when the die is thrown, a universe is actualized for each of its outcomes.

For instance, suppose your die is two-sided, like a coin. The first time you throw it, you do not select only one outcome. Rather, you make two universes: one in which it comes up H (heads) and another in which it comes up T (tails). Each universe is possible. In each of these universes, you throw the die again. There are now 4 universes: HH, HT, TH, TT. In each of these universes, you throw the die again to get 8 universes: HHH, HTH, HTH, HTT, THH, THT, TTH, TTT. For every possible sequence of throws, there is some universe whose history is that sequence. No sequence is excluded from possibility. For Nietzsche, no sequence is excluded from actuality.

The will to power throws the die without limit. It throws all possible sequences; these sequences are infinite into the past and future. All possible sequences of throws strive for actuality and achieve it. The will to power would not be omnipotent if it were morally constrained to select only one sequence for actualization. The will to power is morally compelled to select all sequences for actualization.

When Leibniz's God throws the die, only one side can come up, that is, one possibility gets to be actualized. Leibniz's God doesn't throw the die, but selects one side and puts the die down on that side. The dice game is the complete actualization of all possible universes, all possible sequences of events *without selection according to any rule:* it is chance as the absence of any negative moral principle that would exclude some possible universe from actuality.

9. The World and its Universes

One way to visualize the world is to think of it as a game. Consider the game of chess. In chess there are 32 different pieces. There are "blank" pieces that really occupy apparently empty squares (when you type some text, you have to type the blanks: the blank is not the absence of a character, it's a character in its own right). There are 64 squares on the chess board. An event in the game of chess puts one piece on one square at one instant. A spatial combination of events puts some pieces on some squares at one instant. A spatio-temporal combination of events is a series of spatial combinations.

Considered simply as a spatio-temporal system, every sequence of combinations of pieces is some possible way to play chess. After all, you don't have to play by the standard rules. The standard rules of chess define only one way to arrange pieces in space and to move them in time. There are non-standard rules that define other ways to play chess, and there's nothing logically impossible about playing by those non-standard rules. In fact, it's often lots of fun to make up variants of the standard rules and to play non-standard games.

The *world* of chess contains *all possible* spatial arrangements and *all possible* temporal sequences of spatial arrangements. The world of chess, considered as a purely spatio-temporal system of all possible combinations of chess pieces, is not limited by any system of rules. Indeed, every system of rules involving chess pieces and the chess board has some games in the chess world (including the system of rules that says there are no rules). Once you decide on a system of rules, you can select all the games in the chess world that satisfy those rules. Any collection of such games is a chess universe in the chess world.

Rules for games are like natural laws: they are like the physical rules that specify how physical objects interact in space and time. Of course, these rules are aesthetic fictions. Since the world contains all possible combinations of events, it contains some combination for any consistent system of natural laws. Every combination of events that satisfies some system of natural laws is the space-time history of some physical universe. Just as systems of rules pick out collections of games (space-time histories) from the chess world, so systems of natural laws pick out collections of space-time histories from the world itself. Each of those collections is a whole physical universe.

The world is not this universe or any other universe. The world is much greater than any universe, because every universe is some *particular* spatio-temporal combination of events. Universes are the largest physically possible combinations of events. Since there are many possible ways to combine events into physical wholes, there are many possible universes in the world. Nietzsche's world as will to power is not limited by any particular system of natural laws. The world as will to power contains all possible universes.

10. Freedom and Destiny

Nietzsche's conception of the divine dice game leads implies that he is a *determinist*. All events in our lives are determined by fate, by destiny, by the particular physical universe in which we exist. Nietzsche denies *free will*.[9] To deny free will is not to deny *freedom*. The Roman Stoic philosopher Seneca says the wise person "escapes necessity because he wills what necessity is going to force on him"; and that "fate leads the willing, but drags the unwilling."[10] We are *free to be ourselves* because we *necessarily are* ourselves:

> Over one man *necessity* stands in the shape of his passions, over another as the habit of hearing and obeying, over a third as a logical conscience, over a fourth as caprice and a mischievous pleasure in escapades. These four will, however, seek the *freedom* of their will precisely where each of them is most firmly fettered: it is as if the silkworm sought the freedom of its will in spinning. (WS 9)

Nietzsche says that everything in the world (in any physical universe) has some destiny or fate. The destiny of everything in the world is to be in some particular universes and not others. Nietzsche says that every person has some destiny: "The fatality of [one's] nature cannot be disentangled from the fatality of all that which has been and will be. . . . One is necessary, one is a piece of fate, one belongs to the whole, one *is* in the whole." (TI 6:8)

Nietzsche's parable of the waterfall makes his idea of destiny clear. The parable uses the fiction of an all-knowing mind able to calculate the whole future (and past) of any particular universe:

> At the sight of a waterfall we think we see in the countless curvings, twistings and breakings of the waves capriciousness and freedom of will; but everything here is necessary, every motion mathematically calculable. So it is too in the case of human actions; if one were all-knowing, one would be able to calculate every individual action . . . the actor himself, to be sure, is fixed in the illusion of free will; if for one moment the wheel of the world were to stand still, and there were an all-knowing, calculating intelligence there to make use of this pause, it could narrate the future of every creature to the remotest ages and describe every track along which this wheel had yet to roll. The actor's deception regarding himself,

the assumption of free-will, is part of the mechanism it would have to compute. (HH I:106)

The parable of the waterfall and the wheel of the world presents what looks like a very Newtonian view of the world. Indeed, the all-knowing mind is *Laplace's Demon*, named after the mathematician who worked out many of the details of Newton's physics. But the universe is not Newtonian for Nietzsche, since at every point in the history of the universe all possible alternatives are actualized. The Newtonian universe is both deterministic and singular. It has only one past and future. Both Newton and Leibniz would agree that there is one actual universe. Nietzsche would not.

You and I are not all-knowing minds. We don't know which possible universe we are actually in. We don't know how the next throw of the dice will turn out for us. We are ignorant of our destinies.

11. That Yes Than Which No Greater is Possible

Nietzsche explicitly compares Heraclitus with Leibniz: "Heraclitus after all had no reason why he had to prove (as Leibniz did) that this is the best of all possible worlds. It is enough for him that it is the beautiful innocent game of time (the *aeon*)." (PTG 7, p. 63)

Nietzsche's will to power is Leibniz's doctrine of the striving possibles without the moral negativity of the Christian-Platonic God. Instead, Nietzsche asserts that the will to power drives every striving to its goal of actuality. All possible universes are actual. From this point in time, all possible futures and pasts branch out. The will to power is a divine Yes! to every one of them. The problem for us is that we do not know exactly which possible universe we are in. We know that there are many future possibilities for ourselves, but we do not know what fate will do to us. We do not know our destinies.

Nietzsche says the only way to live with this uncertainty is to affirm all possible universes. Nietzsche refers to this absolute affirmation as the *Dionysian-tragic way of life*. This way of life is tragic because it affirms pain and suffering. Tragedy is not masochism. You don't have to enjoy pain to affirm it. Suppose you have a toothache. I had one once that hurt so severely I collapsed and lay on the floor for an hour. Nietzsche isn't saying you're going to enjoy that. The question is: what attitude do you take to it? No matter what your attitude, it's still going to hurt. The ascetic response to pain is to condemn the universe and life to demand compensation in heaven.

Leibniz's Christian theodicy argues that this is the best of all possible universes. Nietzsche's *Dionysian theodicy* affirms all universes.

It is both tragic and aesthetic: existence is justified aesthetically (BT 5, 24; GS 54; WP 416, 1019). The world is a drama. As such, it is evaluated by its dramatic qualities: its emotional intensity, its beauty. A world without suffering or tragedy is a world without passion; it is a sterile and ugly world. Every universe in the world is like the staging of a play. There are plays of great drama, great pleasure and pain, great emotions. To exclude any drama reduces the beauty of the whole. It makes the whole emotionally flatter. As a tragic-aesthetic theodicy, Nietzsche's view closely recalls the theodicy of Plotinus.[11]

The Dionysian-tragic response is to say Yes! to pain and suffering. Just because pain hurts doesn't make it *evil*. Pain is a great stimulus to life: I hurt therefore I am. So far from condemning any possible universe, the Dionysian-tragic attitude affirms even *the worst of all possible universes*. It celebrates its hell with its heaven. Nietzsche's name for this celebration is *love of fate* (*amor fati*):

> My formula for greatness in a human being is *amor fati:* that one wants nothing to be other than it is, not in the future, not in the past, not in all eternity. Not merely to endure that which happens out of necessity, still less to pretend it isn't real -- but to love it. (EH 3:10; GS 276)

Instead of ascetic supernaturalism, Nietzsche advocates the love of fate. Another name for amor fati is *fatalism* -- the affirmation of one's involvement in fate. A person who sees that his or her destiny or fate is not separate from the destiny of the whole "stands in the midst of the universe with a joyful and trusting fatalism, in the faith that only what is separate and individual may be rejected, that in the totality everything is redeemed and affirmed -- *he no longer denies* . . . But such a faith is the highest of all possible faiths: I have baptized it with the name *Dionysus*" (TI 9:49)

The first step toward a Dionysian-tragic celebration of all universes is to celebrate the universe in which you actually live, whichever one it might be. The goal is a "Dionysian affirmation of the world as it is, without subtraction, exception, or selection" (WP 1041). The way to do this is to affirm this moment. To affirm right here right now:

> If we affirm one single moment, we thus affirm not only ourselves but all existence. For nothing is self-sufficient, neither in us ourselves nor in things; and if our soul has trembled with happiness and sounded like a harp string just once, all eternity was needed to produce this one event -- and in this single moment of affirmation all eternity was called good, redeemed, justified (WP 1032).

Endnotes.

1. Leibniz's influence on Nietzsche is well-known. In his *Nietzsche*, W. Kaufmann describes Nietzsche's philosophy of nature as his "monadology." See A. Moles, *Nietzsche's Philosophy of Nature and Cosmology* (New York: Peter Lang, 1990), pp. 167-172.
2. There are no atoms or beings (BGE 12; WP 552, 624, 636, 704). The will to power is a plenum of events (WP 520, 521, 548-552, 635). It is a set of deeds without doers (BGE 17; TI 3:5; WP 484, 488, 531, 548, 631). Events occur; they don't exist.
3. If any combination of events can occur, it has occurred and it will occur again (Z 3:2/2; WP 1066); no rule constrains the spatio-temporal combination of events (Z III:4, 3:16/3).
4. All citations of Darwin are from C. Darwin, *The Origin of Species* (New York: Penguin Books, 1985). Originally published in 1859.
5. See C. Shields, "Leibniz's Doctrine of the Striving Possibles" *Journal of the History of Philosophy 24* (3) (1986), pp. 343-57; D. Blumenfeld, "Leibniz's Theory of the Striving Possibles" *Studia Leibnitiana 5* (2) (1973), pp. 163-77.
6. N. Rescher, *G. W. Leibniz's Monadology: An Edition for Students* (Pittsburgh, PA: University of Pittsburgh Press, 1991), p. 171.
7. N. Rescher, *G. W. Leibniz's Monadology*, p. 188.
8. Nietzsche uses combinatorial arguments to justify recurrence. If you combine those with his notion of the dice game and absolute affirmation, then all possible combinations of events are actual.
9. HH I:18, 39, 99, 102; AOM 33, 50; GS 110, 345; BGE 18, 19, 21, 53; TI 6:3.
10. Seneca, *Letters from a Stoic*, p. 105.
11. Plotinus, *Enneads*, III.2.15-18. Plotinus's ascetic supernaturalism is not very consistent with his own theory of human being.

5

Herd and Individual

1. The Human Animal

Nietzsche thinks about people biologically. He recognizes that human beings are herd animals -- like horses, sheep, bees, ants, or any other social animal. People are not solitary animals. People live together in social organizations. These facts are so obvious they are easy to ignore. Nietzsche takes them seriously. He uses these biological facts of the human species to develop his moral and political theories.

In many respects, Nietzsche's moral and political ideas are inspired by Darwin's theory of evolution, which was based on the ideas of competition, variation, and survival of the fittest. But Nietzsche is not a social darwinist. He knows that even if those who survive are the fittest, that does not mean they are the best.

2. Mediocrity and Excess

Nietzsche contrasts the human herd with the human individual. The herd and individual are often contrasted as the rule and exception, so that the individuals are exceptional human beings. One good way to think of the contrast is in terms of darwinian evolution: the herd is the human species; the individuals are the variations or mutations.

Every human being has two aspects: his or her *species-being* and his or her *individuality*. Species-being is what each one of us shares in common with all other human beings: it is the generic aspect of our humanity. It is what makes us normal or average. It is what makes us want to fit in. Individuality is deviation or abnormality. In some cases, deviance is functional degeneracy: it is perverse; in other cases, deviance is functional excellence -- the superior athlete, the genius, and the noble leader are not average, they are above average.

Individuals grow out of the herd. They deviate *from* the herd. They are exceptional members *of* the herd. They may come to oppose the organization of the herd, but they never escape it. Individuality is a *modification of* herd-being. All people are social animals.

Nietzsche's contrast between the herd and individual is often linked with values: the herd is *mediocre*, the individuals are *excessive*. The herd is the mean (it is the average), the individuals are extreme. The excess is positive or negative; the average is neutral.

Nietzsche is on the side of the individuals, since he thinks that the biological forces that make human culture excellent and more vital are at work in them (HH I:224). He thinks they are more fragile, since they do not have the protection of the herd. (BGE 268)

Unfortunately, Nietzsche's theory of the herd and individual is easy to misunderstand, and has been abused to justify the worst tyrannies and most degenerate forms of politics.

3. Consciousness as Herd Instinct in the Individual

Here's one way to test whether you're a member of the human herd: are you conscious? are you self-conscious? If the answer is yes to either, then you're a member of the herd. Consciousness is the kind of mental functioning that is natural for herd animals.

Nietzsche offers an evolutionary argument that consciousness is herd instinct in the individual (GS 354). His basic principle is Darwinian: consciousness must have some biological utility, it must have some survival-value. He observes that herd animals are interdependent. Solitary animals are able to survive on their own, but herd animals need assistance from one another. To gain assistance, they have to be able to communicate. To communicate, they have to know their needs. To know their needs, they have to be aware of themselves. So, they have to be conscious and self-conscious:

> Consciousness is really only a net of communication between human beings; it is only as such that it had to develop; a solitary human being who lived like a beast of prey would not have needed it. . . . It was only as a social animal that man acquired self-consciousness. . . . consciousness does not really belong to man's individual existence but rather to his social or herd nature; . . . it has developed subtlety only insofar as this is required by social or herd utility. (GS 354)

So Nietzsche ultimately defines the relation between the herd and the individual in terms of thought: conformity to the herd-standard is ultimately submission to a style or way of thinking. It is a kind of narrow-mindedness or closed-mindedness. The individual mind is exceptional because it is able to think beyond the confines of herd-mentality. The individual is one who has *new thoughts*, who creates *new values*. You can see that Nietzsche defines the relation between herd and individual as a *philosophical relation*.

4. Language as Herd Instinct in the Individual

Since consciousness is intimately associated with communication, it is intimately associated with *language* (GS 354; BGE 268). Words are herd-signals. Language evolves because a herd whose members are able to coordinate their actions via communication is more likely to survive than a herd that is uncoordinated. Nietzsche thinks that language is essentially instinctive, that it emerges via unconscious biological forces in herd-animal species:

> Language is neither the conscious work of individuals nor of a plurality. All conscious thought is possible only with the help of language. . . . Language is much too complex to be the work of a single individual, much too unified to be the work of a mass; it is a complete organism. The only alternative is to consider language to be the product of an instinct, like among the bees.[1]

Since language consists of herd-signals, it is almost impossible to express any uniquely individual insight or thought linguistically. Any thought that emerges into consciousness has already been translated into herd-signs. Language itself censors individuality. Any thought expressed in language is already socially acceptable. The prison-walls that the herd-mind places around thought are not made of stone, but of words, of grammar.

The individual is one who has found a way out in thought, but to be successful as a person (as a social animal) he or she must also find a way out in speech or in communication. Nietzsche thinks that artists are able to do this. By "artist" Nietzsche does not mean painter; he has in mind all the art forms: music, sculpture, architecture, poetry, and so on. The problem is that the artistic ability to escape from the bonds of language is rarely coupled with the kind of rationality that is needed to produce enduring conceptual structures -- but when the artistic inventiveness, scientific rationality, and practical wisdom all coincide in a person's mind and character, that person can change the herd. So far, for almost all of human history, such coincidences have been random. What Nietzsche hopes for is that the human herd will come to organize itself so that individuals are produced deliberately; in this way, human evolution can be enhanced. Since the problem of how to enhance human evolution is one of thought and language (for these are the *human* attributes), it is a *philosophical problem.*

5. Social Conventions

Every animal has some distinctive feature that enables it to survive. For herd animals, the distinctive feature is *herd coordination.* For human animals, herd coordination is especially important since people have very few natural defensive or offensive weapons. We do not have claws or powerful teeth; we do not have thick skins or scales and we are not able to run fast or to fly away. Intelligence is biologically useful for herd animals like us only insofar as it enables us to project goals that exceed the powers of the solitary person and to coordinate our actions toward such great common goals. Science, for instance, is a social enterprise in which the progress of even the genius presupposes the progress of the scientific community.

Herd animals like human beings are fragile precisely because they lack natural defensive and offensive weapons for the evolutionary struggle. So, human beings are greatly endangered animals: "The greater the danger is, the greater is the need to reach agreement quickly and easily" (BGE 268). Rapid and reliable communication is essential for human survival. Misunderstanding is death.

Nietzsche argues that unanimous agreement by the herd on norms and standards that are binding for all has the greatest survival value. Such agreement must be enforced strictly and without exception: for any deviation from the common norm or standard increases the risk of misunderstanding, hence the risk of death for each and all: "man's greatest labor so far has been to reach agreement about very many things and to submit to a law of agreement -- regardless of whether these things are true or false." (GS 76)

The herd-agreement is good; anything else is evil. The herd-norm is a social convention. Herd-norms are initially arbitrary. Their value does not lie in their accuracy or objectivity, but in the fact that they are universally binding for all herd members. Language is a herd-norm (Truth & Lies in Non-moral Sense; GS 354; BGE 268). Morality is also a herd-norm.

Initially, agreement has greater survival value than truth. Initially, to be incorrect together has greater biological utility than to be correct alone. As soon as the herd has enough power to secure its basic bio-logical needs, truth gains survival value. (GS 110)

6. Morality as Herd Instinct in the Individual

Morality, like language, is an example of herd-agreement. Nietzsche does not think there are any objective moral facts. He argues that there are only moral judgments, and that their only value is their relation to the biological enhancement of the human species.

For Nietzsche, all morality is social convention. Morality does not come from God or from nature. Moral codes are like languages: they serve to unify and coordinate the members of a herd. Moralities are, initially, bound up with particular herds: every clan, tribe, or soci-ety has its own moral code. Moral codes reflect the concrete practices of the particular herd: they are systems of *customs*, not abstract princi-ples (HH I:96).

Herd-morality (the morality of customs) does not consist of a list of commands and prohibitions -- of "Thou shalt"s and "Thou shalt not"s. Rather, herd-morality it is a system of traditional or customary ways of being human. It defines the pattern of life for every member of the herd. Herd-morality defines the stages on life's way for males and females, young and old, rich and poor. It defines everybody's social role and obligations in the herd-structure. Morality is the presence of the herd in the action of the individual:

> Wherever we encounter a morality, we also encounter valuations and an order of rank of human impulses and actions. These valua-tions and orders of rank are always expressions of the needs of a community and herd . . . Morality trains the individual to be a function of the herd and to ascribe value to himself only as a func-tion. Morality is herd instinct in the individual. (GS 116)

7. The Natural History of Morals

Nietzsche thinks that humanity began in a state of animal savagery in which the only law was the darwinian law of the jungle: might makes right. But that law is the most inefficient way to exercise power; it is the lowest evolutionary level of the political will to power, because it cannot create or sustain cooperatives. The rule that "Might makes right" is a principle of weakness. The unregulated struggle for existence is a war of all against all. The English philosopher Thomas Hobbes describe that as a condition of universal violence in which life was "nasty, brutish, and short".

Nietzsche thinks that powerful individuals lead the way out of the savage war of all against all. Those potent individuals are the rulers and masters: they are vigorous warlords who stop the struggle of all against all by imposing law and order. Initially, the war of all versus all is stopped by the greater violence and savagery of the warlord. Nietzsche knows well enough that people do not want to obey any laws (else there would not have to be laws), and that for primitive humans the law has to be backed up with violent punishments. At the dawn of human civilization, these warlords are the individuals.

At the start of human civilization, the individuals are all dictators, that is, they are all tyrants or despots -- but some are more enlightened than others. All rule by their egos, but the less enlightened think of their ego as extending no further than their bodies or families, while the more enlightened think of their ego as including the whole group they rule. The more enlightened appear less self-centered, but that is just because they think of the whole community as part of their selves. The less enlightened rule by fiat and arbitrary caprice; the more enlightened seek to preserve the whole community and so they lay down laws to secure harmony and order.

The enlightened despots are the great law-givers. Law is made by humans for humans. It is not made by any gods. Nietzsche deeply admires great law-givers: Moses, Hammurabi, Manu, Solon, the great Pharoahs, the noble Roman Emperors. By an extension of an ego that seeks greater power, the warlord becomes the law-giver. The law-giver is the next stage in the spiritual progress of the individual, and the lawfully ordered civil society is the next stage of the herd.

8. Master & Slave Moralities

Nietzsche thinks that the distinction between those who command and those who obey is natural for animals like humans: "as long as there have been human beings, there have also been herds of men (clans, communities, tribes, peoples, states, churches) and always a great many people who obeyed, compared with the small number of those commanding." (BGE 199)

Nietzsche is famous for his distinction between master moralities and slave moralities. (HH 45; BGE 260; GM 1) What is often overlooked is his view that both master and slave moralities are primitive relics lower human cultures. On the way to higher culture, the opposition of master and slave morality must be left behind. They are human, all-too-human, and "Man must be overcome."

Master morality originates with the rulers. The rulers determine what is good. Most importantly, they conceive of themselves as the creators of values and laws. They are proud of themselves; they are honorable, they keep their promises, and they do not lie. (BGE 260; GM 2) The masters refer to themselves as *good* and to the slaves as *bad*. Nietzsche says that bad is not the same as evil. Bad means contemptible, cowardly, vengeful, unreliable, dysfunctional.

Master morality is an ethic of overflowing power. First and foremost, it is an ethic of self-control and self-rule. The master is one who has control over his or her own emotions and passions. Mastery always starts with self-master, not with mastery over others. The masters honor one another, and they help others who are less fortunate not out of pity but because to help is to exercise power. The masters are generous, not stingy. They give away because they have plenty and are not afraid of getting more. The masters respect one another, but they do not respect their social inferiors. Master morality is an ethic of virtue, of striving for excellence, of the will to be the best. The masters do not suffer when they feel pain: they endure it. Masters do not hate their enemies, because they respect and honor them. Masters are grateful and vengeful. They requite and retaliate.

Slave morality is different. Slave morality is a morality of pity, of compassion out of fear of suffering. It is a morality that originates in cowardice and indecision. The slave, Nietzsche says, does not have any self-control, but merely reacts to stimuli. Slaves are petty and mean, so their morality is one of petty utility. Humility and self-negation (not self-sacrifice) are aspects of slave morals. Because slaves are parasites, they value flattery; because they are too weak or cowardly to fight an honest open fight, they value dirty tricks and sneaky craftiness. Resentment and passive aggression are praised by slave morality. While the slaves call themselves *good*, they call the masters *evil*. Slave morality is a morality of fear.

9. Christian Morality as Slave Morality

Nietzsche thinks that Christian morality is the worst of all possible slave moralities. Compared with the great moral systems of Greece and Rome, Christian morality is degenerate and sick. It has nothing positive or beneficial to offer.

You might say that Nietzsche is wrong because Christian morality has done a great deal of good: there are many social benefits, such as the care for the sick and poor. Nietzsche counters that there is nothing especially Christian about that: Jews, Muslims, Buddhists, Hindus, Roman and Greek pagans, and even atheists all stress the value of helping others to build a strong and well-ordered community.

The Christian worships not God, but his or her own ego (soul). The Christian is a Christian solely out of selfishness: due to the reward in heaven. Moreover, the Christian does nothing to earn this reward, but simply gets it for no work -- something only a slave would enjoy. The Christian wants to see his or her enemies tortured forever in hell: slave resentment at its finest. Of course, as Nietzsche is fond of pointing out, this is all imaginary. The slave is not able to injure his or her enemies here, not able to enjoy anything good due to his or her own work here, so he or she imagines a world in the future someplace else in which he or she gets something that he or she does not even deserve or merit on earth.

The master/slave distinction has never disappeared, it just becomes more refined. As far as Nietzsche is concerned, modern industrial-corporate society is just a highly refined form of slavery. Nietzsche declares that the modern factory worker or office worker (who seems free) is as much a slave as anyone in chains.

10. Justice and Cooperation among Peers

In any conflict there are two alternatives: one side is more powerful than the other, or the two sides have similar power. In the first case, the struggle ends quickly with one side the victor and the other the loser. This is, Nietzsche thinks, the classical pattern of survival of the fittest in the evolutionary struggle for existence. But the second case is more important, especially for social animals like people.

In any struggle between two equally matched opponents, the result is likely to be a mutually destructive clash with no clear winner. So for each side the risk of self-destruction is great, while the benefit of victory is small. In this case, it is better for each side to form a union with the other side, to negotiate, to find something in common, and to cooperate. If the two competitors can become cooperators, the result is a pair that is stronger than either of them, that is then able to go on to greater victories. Cooperation has a clear survival-value in the struggle for existence. Nietzsche is explicit: cooperation emerges not from any altruistic motives, not from any love of the other, but from pure self-interest: unbridled egotistical lust for domination is what creates all cooperative social organization. (HH I:92)

Indeed, Nietzsche thinks that fairness emerges from unfairness and justice originates from injustice. This is part of his thesis that higher values emerge from lower values (BGE 2; TI 3). As equally balanced forces learn to cooperate, justice and fairness are necessary. Neither side wants to risk offending the other by any sort of unfair dealing. Each side takes care to respect the needs of the other side, since each side respects the power of the other side. Justice and fairness come from mutual respect, but that presupposes a balance of power. It is in the self-interest of parties of equal power to treat one another as equals, to accord to one another equal rights. (HH I:451).

11. The Will to Power and Political Organization

One of the most senseless misunderstandings of Nietzsche's idea of the will to power is that Nietzsche endorses a politics of oppression: the masters are supposed to oppress or to dominate the slaves.

In any group in which one faction oppresses or dominates another, power is not increased; rather, power is wasted. If a master has to dominate or to oppress his or her slaves, the master is wasting his or her own power and the slaves are wasting their power. The power of each side is wasted in its struggle against the other. Oppression and domination are inefficient ways to generate more power.

A couple with two equally powerful hence mutually respectful and cooperating partners is more powerful overall than a couple in which a stronger partner oppresses a weaker partner. A society in which men oppress women, or in which one racial, ethnic, or religious group oppresses another, is a very weak society. Such a collective is torn apart internally; it's internal frictions will lead to its self-destruction in civil war or internal violence. Nietzsche thinks such social groups are like sick bodies rather than like healthy bodies. In a healthy body, all the organs cooperate harmoniously.

The will to power aims beyond social systems in which one group oppresses or dominates another, since such systems are wasteful and inefficient -- in the evolutionary competition for existence with other more harmoniously organized social systems, the internally divided systems will lose and be destroyed. The will to power aims to make an ordered and peacefully functioning unity out of every warring or competitive multiplicity, because a coherently ordered system of cooperative parts is stronger than a system with internal struggle.

Nietzsche does not therefore deny that the more powerful *impose* on the less powerful. The most important task of the powerful masters is to impose *order*, to impose *laws*. The task of the masters is to end the chaotic anarchy of the war of all against all by devising and then by aggressively enforcing laws codes. Such aggressive enforcement is often bloody and violent: rebellions must be put down, outlaw bands must be destroyed, ethnic feuds and hatreds must be halted.

In any collective, the danger is revenge. Small accidental offenses can trigger tit-for-tat blood feuds between families, gangs, religious or ethical factions. This is the negative side of the conflict among approximately equal powers: instead of agreeing to cooperate, they fight a long, drawn-out and hopeless war of mutual attrition, a cycle of hatred in which every act is a retaliation or reaction. This is the reactive trap in which the political will to power can be caught. If no stronger power intervenes, the cycle of violence can go on forever.

Nietzsche is clear that justice obtains only when the stronger imposes law and order to quiet the reactive hatreds of the weaker:

> Wherever justice is practiced and maintained, we see a stronger power intent on finding means to regulate the senseless raging of rancor among its weaker subordinates. This is accomplished by . . . devising, proposing, and if necessary *enforcing* compromises, or by setting up a normative scale of equivalents for damages . . . But, above all, by the establishment of a code of laws which the superior power imposes upon the forces of hostility and resentment. (GM 2:11)

Morality begins as *compulsion*: the individuals (masters) compel the herd (slaves) to obey laws. But then compulsion becomes *custom*, as compulsion produces habitual behaviors. (HH I:97) Then morality begins to become subtle and rational. Moral philosophies appear.

Historically, Nietzsche recognizes that the struggle for existence within and between social groups is violent and savage. He knows that human history is mainly the history of barbarism, since that's the longest period of human existence. We are not so far from the animals. He does not deny that, historically, mastery is exercised by cruelty and brutality. But he also argues that human history is one in which there is *spiritual progress:* cruelty becomes refined (BGE 229, 230).

According to Nietzsche, the golden rule "Do unto others as you would have them do unto you," is sheer self-interest. However, it is self-interest that has made spiritual progress, that has found its way past the earlier and weaker principle of "Might makes right." The Golden Rule is *enlightened self-interest.* Nietzsche does not ever think that human beings, which are animals, will ever progress beyond self-interest. All that can happen is that their self-interest can become increasingly enlightened, increasingly wise and spiritualized. It can become more thoughtful, more *philosophical.*

12. Noble and Servile Characters

The contrast herd and individual is often confused with the contrast between master and slave. Master and slave are ethical categories for Nietzsche. Master and slave are not legal categories. So, masters may be legally bound and may be forced to labor in chains under the cruel whips of slaves. Sometimes slaves dominate masters. Master and slave are really types of character. Nietzsche also refers to these character-types as noble versus base, active versus reactive, healthy versus sick, and affirmative versus negative.

There is a slave-herd and a master-herd; there are slave-individuals and master-individuals. The master/slave contrast is not the same as the powerful/powerless contrast. Slaves are able to gain political power and to dominate. Tyrants are slaves with political power, and political orders based wholly on tyranny, like fascism, are political orders in which there are no masters at all.

It's unfortunate that Nietzsche uses terms like "master" and "slave". Today the ugly connotations of these words make Nietzsche's ideas open to easy abuses and misunderstandings. The terms that serve his purposes better are "noble" and "servile".

Sometimes Nietzsche contrasts *retarded* and *anticipatory* persons, and that contrast serves his purposes better since it evaluates types of persons relative to their place in human evolutionary history:

> The unpleasant character who is full of mistrust, consumed with envy whenever competitors or neighbors achieve a success, and violently opposes all opinions not his own, demonstrates that he belongs to an earlier stage of culture and is thus a relic: for the way in which he traffics with men was the apt and right one for conditions obtaining during an age of club-law; he is a retarded man. Another character who readily rejoices with his fellow men, wins friends everywhere, welcomes everything new and developing, takes pleasure in the honors and successes of others and makes no claim to be in the sole possession of the truth but is full of a diffident mistrust -- he is an anticipatory man striving towards a higher human culture. (HH I:614)

13. Spiritual Progress from Lower to Higher Culture

As human society makes spiritual progress in its moral systems and political organization, it depends less and less on savage domination and more and more on the harmonious balancing of opposed powers, of claims and counterclaims:

> For wherever grand cultural architecture has developed, its purpose has been to effect a harmony and concord between contending powers through the agency of an overwhelming assemblage of the other powers, but without the need to suppress them or clap them in

irons. (HH I:276, cf. 278)

As humanity makes spiritual progress from lower culture to higher culture, leaders are needed who are able to arrange powers into the harmonious order in which purposive cooperation is maximal and the inefficiency of internal struggle is minimal. Such leaders are artists of political power and moral order. The products of their artistic creation are social systems. They are like architects, since they have to create stable enduring structures; they are like musicians or sculptors, since they have to build their stable structures out of the plastic material that is human desire, and this can only be done through harmony. They are a supremely enlightened type of law-giver. Nietzsche calls these enlightened leaders *superhumans*.

Nietzsche is not in favor of rational *social engineering:* humanity is far too complex and too irrational for it to be successfully forced into simple rational structures. Nietzsche would certainly have predicted the demise of Communist states, in which everything was planned by centralized bureaucracies. In accordance with his darwinian outlook, Nietzsche advocates *social experimentalism.* (BGE 223) Natural selection will sort out the successes from the failures.

The 19th century was an age of great social experimentation. Many utopian communities were founded by men and women with novel ideas about how people should live together. Of course, in order to have social experiments, it is necessary to have *experimenters:* those who are able to think up new forms of social organization and those who are willing to try to live accordingly. In evolutionary terms, it is necessary to have deviations or mutations in order for the species to advance (HH I:224). The experimenters are exceptional individuals whose life-patterns differ from the homogeneous life-patterns of the herd. They are *attempters.* (BGE 42) They are *spiritual pioneers.* But Nietzsche fears that society is becoming so deeply herd-like that it will stamp out anyone with a different way of living, so that the experimenters will disappear.

14. The Free Spirit and the Bound Spirit

Ancient societies were characterized by explicit and savage forms of mastery and slavery. Among the Greeks and Romans, these became more civil, more subtle, more refined. In the Middle Ages, master and slave relations became the lord and serf relations of feudalism: both lord and serf were bound by codes of mutual obligation. In the modern age, the master-slave relation became economic: the master is the employer or boss, the slave is the employee or worker. In his own day,

Nietzsche thinks this relation has become very spiritual and refined: the slave is *the bound spirit*, the master is the *free spirit.*

While slaves are crudely bound by physical chains or dominated by physical violence, the bound spirit is fettered by mental chains. The chains are more subtle and stronger, since they are made of thought. The bound spirit is not even able to think of freedom, because he or she is not able to think of any other way of living.

Nietzsche is very clear that slavery is an ethical condition: one can be a slave no matter how much money or political power one has: "As at all times, so now too, men are divided into the slaves and the free; for he who does not have two-thirds of his day to himself is a slave, let him be what he may otherwise: statesman, businessman, official, scholar." (HH I:283) Freedom is idleness; it is leisure. But it is not the idleness of lazy passivity or sloth (HH I:284). It is a dynamic idleness, the fertile soil out of which exceptional thoughts grow. In fact, Nietzsche argues that people who seem active because of their constant busyness are often the most spiritually lazy -- for they do not ever take the time to form their own opinions, to work out their own uniquely personal salvation from averageness of thought. The rich banker remains a slave to money and does not bother to ask why wealth is valuable; the powerful politician is a slave to public opinion or his or her own ego and does not bother to ask why such power is valuable. Such is the laziness of the active (HH I:286).

Spiritual bondage is conceptual and habitual. Enduring habits that are deeply entrenched in a person's character are spiritual bonds (GS 295). Spiritual bondage is bondage to customs, people, institutions, technologies. For example, spiritual bonds are the ties that bind us to a profession, to a corporation or business, to a spouse or family, to money or to status, to a political party or ideology, to a religious sect, to diet, to addictions, to sickness, to the past whether of the self or of social tradition, or to a daily routine, to public opinion. (HH I:229).

To the extent that one thinks that one *has to* work for a corporation at a 9-5 job, that one *has to* have a house in the suburbs, that one *has to* be a consumer, that one *has to* have a nuclear family, that one *has to* have a car, that there is *no other way* to work, to live, to get around, one is a spiritual slave. Nietzsche's point is that there are other ways, there are necessarily other ways.

Ultimately, the free spirit thinks differently, does not conform to herd-conventions (HH I:225) The free spirit is one who is willing to take risks, who does not fear failure. To survive, the free spirit needs great resourcefulness and regenerative power, since the free spirit lives dangerously (GS 283). The free spirit tries out different ways of living. The free spirit does not want to get stuck in a rut, but is restless and dynamic. The free spirit has brief habits (GS 295). The free spirit experiments with his or her daily routine, always striving for nobility, that is, to maximize his or her creative potency (GS 22, 308) The free spirit experiments with all aspects of his or her life, always striving for the optimal conditions of his or her unique health (HH I:286; see GM 3:7 on optimality)

The problem of modernity is that the slaves (bound spirits) have all the power; the masters (free spirits) have none. It is the complete victory of the herd over the individual. Those who command, in the sense of those who lead by creating new values and new possibilities for humanity, are lacking: "the herd instinct of obedience is inherited best, and at the expense of the art of commanding. If we imagine this instinct progressing for once to its ultimate excess, then those who command and are independent would eventually be lacking altogether" (BGE 199) Nietzsche thinks that modern society is very close to the complete suppression of anything abnormal or deviant: it defines evil as deviation from the norm. For modern society, every deviant is a pervert, and all must be levelled down to the lowest common denominator. Conformity is ruthlessly enforced.

15. The Superhuman

Nietzsche refers to the effective free spirit as the superhuman. The superhuman is Nietzsche's way of updating the classical concept of the philosophical "wise man" or sage. It is a refinement of Plato's philosopher king, Aristotle's Great-Souled Man, and the Stoic and Epicurean sages. The superhuman has many different appearances. At times, and from different perspectives, the superhuman appears to be a prophet, or a cult leader, or a despot. The superhuman is, as Nietzsche puts it, *beyond good and evil* -- that is, the superhuman is beyond slave morality and the servile way of looking at life.

The superhuman is driven by an extreme will to power and so acts out of self-interest and pure egoism. But the ego of the superhuman is spiritually refined to the point of extreme universality. It is an ego that thinks of itself as containing the whole of humanity, in the sense that its own self-enhancement is the enhancement of every person as far as human history possibly extends into the future.

The superhuman is a human who takes upon himself or herself the responsibility for humanity as a whole, a responsibility humans so far have proven unable to take. This is true mostly, Nietzsche thinks, because we think there is a God who is responsible for us. So we do not bother to take responsibility for ourselves or for the future of our species. The morality of the superhuman is the morality of the mature individual (HH I:95), it is pure self-interest, but that self is the whole self of the whole human species. The superhuman has the most extreme self-control and self-regulation: the self-mastery of the superhuman is sufficient to take responsibility for all humanity.

To understand the superhuman, we need to discuss utilitarianism. The superhuman is a sort of *superutilitarian* agent. Nietzsche often argues against utilitarianism, which views usefulness (utility) as the supreme value. Something is useful insofar as it increases happiness, in the sense of the least pain and greatest pleasure. So utilitarians introduced *the greatest happiness principle:* something is good to the extent that it leads to the greatest happiness of the greatest number of people for the greatest time. Nietzsche's argument against utility is that it is usually reduced to servile herd-utility: what is useful is useful to the herd here and now, for the mere survival of this herd here and now rather than for the enhancement of humanity. The idea that happiness is the least pain and most pleasure is the way a drunkard or drug-addict might view happiness: a kind of stupor or narcotic haze in which true feeling is anesthetized and replaced by a vague and illusory high. Nietzsche despises that.

The superhuman is a superutilitarian because he or she interprets happiness not in the servile sense of least pain and most pleasure, but rather as functional excellence, as optimal performance, as the greatest actualization of all human possibilities. Great athletes, for instance, are willing to suffer great pain to achieve great goals. The superhuman denies that people are sheep or that living in a narcotic stupor is an affirmative way to live. The superhuman has great goals in mind for humanity, and envisions a history full of glorious daring and extraordinary achievements. The superhuman envisions the extreme extension of knowledge and action.

Science and technology have already given humanity great power to build a supercivilization on earth, perhaps to colonize other planets in our solar system, to gain greater knowledge, to become like the gods of which we dreamed in our primitive religions. Yet we hold ourselves back by our bondage to savage superstitions and barbaric illusions, particularly religious faiths. Nietzsche is well-aware that the irrational side of humanity needs satisfaction. He thinks the idea of a grand project for humanity is one in whose glory the irrational side of humanity can be caught up and sublimated.

In order to orient human reason and passion toward great goals, the superhuman practices a kind of enlightened despotism. The base or servile elements of human nature -- human reactivity -- still has to be mastered, and often in crude and brutal ways. Nietzsche has no illusions about the savagery of which people are capable. He knows that the love of the superhuman for humanity is often tough-love:

He would manipulate falsehood, force, the most ruthless self-interest as his instruments so skillfully he could only be called an evil, demonic being; but his objectives, which here and there shine through, would be great and good. He would be centaur, half beast, half man, and with angel's wings attached to his head in addition. (HH I:241)

Even so, the despotism of the superhuman is so highly spiritualized, so philosophical, that it uses as little violent coercion and brutality as possible: it does not aim to suppress or oppress the human beast, but to put that beast to work for a higher goal. The superhuman works by an artistry that both seduces the animal part of human nature and persuades the rational part. The superhuman practices what Nietzsche calls *the joyful wisdom:* a fusion of scientific rationality, practical wisdom, legislative excellence, and art (AOM 180; GS 112).

Nietzsche views modernity as leading to the kinds of crises that will require superhuman intervention. We have to face the fact that our destiny is not determined by God -- God is dead. We need to secure our future on this planet, in this universe; we need to get the human animal under control, to harness our own deep life-power for noble goals. Today, when human recklessness risks destroying the earth for the most petty kind of greed, Nietzsche's ideas are worth looking at closely. We are not doing a very good job of managing our own affairs; we care nothing for future generations or for human destiny. We are engaged in a relentless and blind process of self-destruction, because we are driven by blind biological imperatives to reproduce and consume. The superhuman aims to harness these biological forces for the greatest functional excellence of all humanity.

16. Affirmative Ethics and Politics

Nietzsche desires an affirmative political organization of the whole human species rather than the negative organizations that have so far characterized human politics. He conceives of an organization of the species in which the individuals are free and powerful, and in which they take responsibility for themselves and for the herd -- not in order to enforce herd conformity, but in order to optimize and enhance human possibilities and to achieve the greatest and highest goods for the whole human species. Nietzsche has a utopian view that does not deny human suffering and misfortune, but that uses it as the raw material out of which nobility is sculpted:

My Utopia. -- In a better ordering of society the heavy work and exigencies of life will be apportioned to him who suffers least as a consequence of them, that is to say to the most insensible, and thus step by step up to him who is most sensitive to the most highly sublimated species of suffering. (HH I:462)

Human pain and misfortune can be made meaningful if humanity as a whole is engaged in a great project, one in which all that is human is affirmed. Nietzsche envisages a world and life-affirming political organization whose goal is the greatest functional excellence of all that lives for the longest time. That is his *aristocracy* -- the rule by the best for the best. It remains for us to determine what the best is; but Nietzsche thinks that we can do that only by experimenting with our selves, not blindly or superstitiously, not according to barbaric ideologies, but self-consciously and scientifically.

Endnotes.

1. F. Nietzsche, *On Rhetoric & Language,* trans. S. Gilman et al. (New York: Oxford University Press, 1989), p. 209.

6

Eternal Recurrence

1. Occurrence and Recurrence

One of the most important parts of Nietzsche's philosophy is his idea of *the eternal return of the same*, also called *eternal recurrence*. The easiest way to put it is that everything happens over and over:

> This life as you now live it and have lived it, you will have to live once more and innumerable times more; and there will be nothing new in it, but every pain and every joy and every thought and sigh and everything unutterably small or great in your life will have to return to you, all in the same succession and sequence. (GS 341)

Like many deep philosophical ideas, it sounds outrageous until you start to think about it. As you do think about it, you go into deeper and deeper layers of understanding until you see that the idea has changed from what you first thought it was.

I take the eternal return seriously. I'll leave it to you to decide if it's true or false, but I don't think it's a myth or a joke.[1] I don't think it's poetry or nonsense. Nor do I think it's a physical theory.

The eternal return of the same says something about how reality is ordered. It says something extreme about *occurrence*. It says that reality necessarily repeats itself. It says that every occurrence is a recurrence. The eternal return is about basic logical categories: same and different, one and many, part and whole, simple and complex, concrete and abstract, particular and universal.

The will to power says why there is something rather than nothing; the eternal return says why there is order in that something.

75

Reality is ordered because the will to power repeats itself. The "Yes!" of the will to power is the "Again!" of the eternal return. Together the will to power and the eternal return order absolute affirmation.

2. Recurrence and Immortality

One of the consequences of eternal recurrence is that you and I are immortal, though not continuously. You have infinitely many bodies and lives distributed through eternity. Your lives are interrupted by immense periods of time during which your body doesn't exist, but there's no time before which or after which you don't exist. You'll always exist again. You are born, live, and die infinitely often.

Eternal recurrence is entirely materialistic or physical, since it is your physical body that recurs. There is no immaterial soul or spirit. So in some ways, eternal recurrence resembles the Christian doctrine of the resurrection of the body. The original Christian doctrine of the resurrection stresses the eternal life of the body. It doesn't involve any ghostly soul. But recurrence differs from the Christian doctrine of resurrection, since every recurrent body is mortal, and since there is no moral machinery of judgment that puts your resurrected body in Heaven or Hell. Eternal recurrence happens entirely in this world: there is no other world nor is there any better world (Heaven) nor worse world (Hell). This is it. Recurrence isn't reincarnation, since there's no soul to put into another body (to re-incarnate), and since you recur in the same body you have now. There is no consciousness between occurrences nor memory of previous occurrences. But there is a trivial sense in which you remember your past lives, since they are the same as your present life, and you remember your earlier present life.

Since eternal recurrence implies that you always have a future, it is a theory that can provide some comfort in the face of death. Nietzsche is aware of this, and he thinks that the comfort provided by eternal recurrence is more life affirming than the comfort that other forms of personal immortality provide. To affirm eternal recurrence is to affirm your body and its life in this universe. It isn't ascetic otherworldliness: there is no other universe. This universe is what recurs.

3. Presentations of Eternal Recurrence

Recurrence is an old idea, probably first taught in the West by the Pythagoreans. The ancient Greek philosopher Eudemus stood before his students and said: "If one were to believe the Pythagoreans, with the result that the same individual things will recur, then I shall be talking to you again sitting as you are now, with this pointer in my hand, and everything else will be just as it is now."[2] The idea seems to occur in the Old Testament. Ecclesiastes 1:9 says: "The thing that hath been, it is that which shall be; and that which is done is that which shall be done: and there is no new thing under the sun." Heraclitus and the Stoics also talked about the eternal return. Nietzsche knew about those old versions of recurrence (EH 5:3).

Nietzsche's first discussion of recurrence refers to the Pythagoreans. The Pythagoreans thought of recurrence as the repetition of patterns of physical events within the universe (UM 2, p. 70). Nietzsche *denies* that such physical repetition can ever happen, because: "the dice-game of chance and the future could never again produce anything exactly similar to what it produced in the past" (UM 2, p. 70). The eternal return is a deeper and stranger idea than mere physical repetition.

For awhile, in *Human All-Too-Human* and *Daybreak*, Nietzsche seems to forget about recurrence. The idea reappears in *The Gay Science*, Nietzsche says that "the world is a musical box that eternally repeats its tune, which may never be called a melody" (GS 109). In a section entitled "The Greatest Weight" (GS 341), Nietzsche uses the eternal return to present an ethical dilemma: do you want to live your life over and over again exactly as you have lived it?

In another book, *Thus Spoke Zarathustra*, Nietzsche invents a character named Zarathustra, a wandering philosopher who has many adventures. In one adventure, Zarathustra climbs a mountain and argues with his arch-enemy, a dwarf named the Spirit of Gravity (a spirit of negativity and despair). Zarathustra has a vision of the eternal return:

> Behold this moment!, Zarathustra said. From this gateway [called] Moment, a long, eternal lane runs back: an eternity lies behind us. Must not all things that can run have already run along this lane? Must not all things that can happen have already happened, been done, run past? And if all things have been here before: what do you think of this moment, dwarf? Must not this gateway, too, have been here -- before? And are not all things bound fast together in such way that this moment draws after it all future things? Therefore -- draws itself too? For all things that can run must also run once again forward along this long lane. . . . and I and you at this gateway whispering together, whispering of eternal things -- must we not all have been here before? -- and must we not return and run down that other lane out before us, down that long, terrible lane -- must we not return eternally? (Z 3:2/2)

Later, Zarathustra talks with his animals, an Eagle and a Snake. They tell him that they understand his theory of eternal recurrence:

Behold, we know what you teach: that all things recur eternally and we ourselves with them, and that we have already existed an infinite number of times before and all things with us. You teach that there is a great year of becoming, a colossus of a year: this year must, like an hour-glass, turn itself over again and again, so that it may run down and run out anew: So that all these years resemble one another, in the greatest things and in the smallest, so that we ourselves resemble ourselves in each great year, in the greatest things and in the smallest. And if you should die now, Oh Zarathustra: behold, we know too what you would then say to yourself -- "Now I die and decay" you would say, "and in an instant I shall be nothingness. Souls are as mortal as bodies. But the complex of causes in which I am entangled will recur -- it will create me again! I myself am part of these causes of the eternal recurrence. I shall return, with this sun, with this earth, with this eagle, with this serpent -- not to a new life or a better life or a similar life: I shall return eternally to this identical and self-same life, in the greatest things and in the smallest, to teach once more the eternal recurrence of all things." (Z 3:13/2)

4. Going Through All the Combinations

The classical argument for recurrence is based on combinations. The British philosopher David Hume presents the argument like this:

A finite number of particles is only susceptible of finite transpositions; and it must happen, in an eternal duration, that every possible order or position must be tried an infinite number of times. This world, therefore, with all its events, even the most minute, has before been produced and destroyed, and will again be produced and destroyed, without any bounds and limitations. No one who has a conception of the powers of the infinite, in comparison of the finite, will ever scruple this determination.[3]

Ultimately, in his notebooks of 1888, Nietzsche makes a very similar argument for recurrence based on the combinations of events:

If the world may be thought of as a certain definite quantity of force and as a certain definite number of centers of force ... it follows that, in the great dice game of existence, it must pass through a calculable number of combinations. In infinite time, every possible combination would at some time or another be realized; more: it would be realized an infinite number of times. And since between every combination and its next recurrence all other possible combinations would have to take place, . . . a circular movement of absolutely identical series is thus demonstrated: the world as a circular movement that has already repeated itself infinitely often and plays its dice game in infinitum. (WP 1066)

Nietzsche's arguments for recurrence, both in *Zarathustra* and *The Will To Power* notes, are purely combinatorial. The arguments don't presuppose or depend on any special *physical* facts. The argument in the *Will To Power* assumes only that there are finitely many possible combinations of physical things (centers of force) and that there are infinitely many moments of time. The notions of finite and infinite are mathematical, and the reasoning is also mathematical.

Nietzsche's combinatorial argument from the *Will To Power* rules out one common misinterpretation of eternal recurrence. The argument implies that there is no single special or lucky sequence of events or history of the universe that is selected for recurrence while all others are excluded. Nietzsche says that all combinations occur: all possible sequences of events occur, all possible histories of the universe occur.

All possible histories of our universe occurs infinitely often. So, all possible histories of our solar system, and all possible histories of our earth, occur infinitely often. To make the abstraction personal: every possible history of your body occurs infinitely often. Every one of your possible biographies occurs infinitely often. You don't have just one biography. Nietzsche believes in destiny. Your destiny is to live every life that it is possible for you to live. Your fate is to be and to do all that it is possible for you to be and to do. In such a reality, there is no use for "free will". You are free, because there is nothing you are able to do that you do not do. You are not prohibited from doing anything you are able to do. If that's not freedom, what is? Nietzsche denies "free will" to affirm an even greater freedom, an absolute freedom of the self, an absolute affirmation of the self and the world.

5. Repetition in Games

One way to think about the eternal return in terms of combinations is to think about it in terms of games. Games are activities with clear rules. A game is like a small universe. Nietzsche himself uses the image of the dice game in his arguments for eternal recurrence. The fact that this image is repeated, over and over again, from the start of Nietzsche's career in 1874 to the end in 1888, shows that it is no accident. The will to power is the dice game of recurrence.

A coin is a two-sided die. Probably the simplest dice game you can play is just to flip a coin and write down which side is up when the coin lands. It has to come up heads (H) or tails (T). Suppose you flip it 3 times. If the coin lands heads, then heads, then heads, you write down the series: HHH. There are 8 possible series of 3 flips: HHH, HHT, HTH, HTT, THH, THT, TTH, TTT. You can see that once you flip the coin 3 times, there must be repetition: either H or T *must* recur. It's no accident. It's necessary, because there are only 2 ways for the coin to land, but you've flipped it more than that.

Now suppose you're playing tic-tac-toe with a partner. There are only finitely many games of tic-tac-toe. If you're X you have 9 choices for your first move; if you're O, then you have 8 choices, so there are 9*8 ways to make the first two moves. If you play until all the squares are filled up, there are 9*8*7*6*5*4*3*2*1 = 362,880 different games of tic-tac-toe. That seems like a big number, but it's still finite. If you play 362,881 games of tic-tac-toe, one of those games has to be repeated, move for move. The same game recurs.

You can extend the tic-tac-toe reasoning to chess. Everything about chess is finite. There are finitely many pieces in chess, the size of the board is finite, and the rules say each game has only finitely many moves. There are about 10^{44} different games of chess: a 1 followed by 44 zeroes. That's a big number, but it's finite. If you've played 10^{100} games of chess, you've had to repeat some of the earlier games, move for move. The very same games recur.

Not all games are based on rules. Dice games depend on luck. You throw some dice to determine your moves. Or perhaps moves just happen randomly. You can easily imagine an eternal chess board with 32 eternal chess pieces that move around randomly. This game has no beginning and no end: it goes on infinitely into the past and infinitely into the future. Nothing is created or destroyed in this tiny universe: if pieces of opposite color collide, the captured piece goes to the other side of the board (and if it is captured there, it goes to the other side). Since there are only finitely many pieces and squares, there are only finitely many ways to move pieces around; so some regularity has to appear sometime. There may even be long periods of time during which pieces move according to our rules of chess, even some period during which a whole game of chess is played. So, after very many random re-arrangements, there have to be some repeated configurations of pieces on the board, even some repeated series of configurations, and eventually totally repeated games.

6. Physics Neither Affirms nor Refutes Recurrence

You can agree completely with *any* physical theory and still affirm eternal recurrence. No physical theory either affirms or refutes recurrence, because recurrence *can't possibly be* a physical theory. No physical version of the eternal recurrence of the same goes deep enough, for the same that recurs is the entire physical universe.

Our most perfect physical theory, even the one absolutely perfectly true theory of the physical universe (if there is such a theory) is no more than a theory of *just one thing*, the one single occurrence of the whole spatio-temporal physical universe in which we exist (or of which the theory is true). So that theory is not able to say anything at all about whether or not there are any *other occurrences* of the whole physical universe, since those other occurrences aren't in the physical universe. They are outside of physical space-time.

Of course, there's nothing *physically* outside our universe. But that doesn't mean there's nothing *logically* outside our universe. For all we know, there are many other universes -- real physical things -- that have logical but not physical relations with out universe. Perhaps there are no other universes. But whether there are or not is not a matter to be settled by any physical theory.

The eternal recurrence of the same is not about repetition *in* space and time; it's about the repetition *of* space and time. Recurrence isn't something that happens *in* any universe; recurrence happens *to* every universe. This is why it's a theory of *eternal* recurrence, not *spatio-temporal* recurrence. There is no recurrence *internal* to any universe; recurrence is an *external* relation among universes. It's not a relation among many physical (spatio-temporal) parts of the same universe; it's a non-physical relation between different universes.

7. The Example of the Recurrence of Chess

Any game of chess is like a small universe. Any game of chess takes place on a chess board, which is a small 2-dimensional space. Each square is one unit of space. Any game takes place in time, since one move is made after another. Each move takes one unit of time. The rules of chess are a perfect theory of the game of chess. They define what configurations and moves are possible.

Suppose you are one of the pieces in some chess game. You move from place to place. You are trying to figure out the natural laws of your universe, which are, of course, the rules of chess. You observe how pieces move around on the board; you see how they are captured. After awhile you figure out the rules. You have a true scientific theory of your whole physical space-time. You know that your chess-universe began with a special configuration and evolved through a series of moves. Pawns always move forward, never backward. Pieces go away but never come back. The number of pieces always decreases. You realize that eventually the game will come to an end with checkmate or stalemate. Changes in the chess-universe are not reversible, so the chess-universe has a sort of "arrow of time" that points in one direction, toward the end of the game. Your world is doomed.

Every possible scientific theory you can formulate about the chess-universe depends on observations *made from within* that universe. You can't get physically outside of your own physical space-time to gather any data about that whole space-time from the outside, since there isn't any physical way to get outside of physical reality. So you can't have any *scientific* theory of anything outside of the game. But that doesn't mean there isn't anything outside of the game. There is no possible scientific evidence that there either is or is not anything outside of the game. You can't have a scientific theory, but you can have a philosophical theory. For instance: eternal recurrence.

One thing is certain: your chess-universe isn't embedded in a larger chess-universe. If your chess-universe is embedded in any larger game, that larger game has different rules. Its rules are rules about playing chess games, not about playing chess. For example, one rule might be: after every game, set up the board and play another game; after every game, players switch colors. Those are not rules of chess.

Setting up the board again involves moving pieces back into their initial places. But none of those moves are chess moves. Relative to the time in any chess game, setting up the board takes no time at all. It doesn't happen in the time of chess. For any current game, there always is a *previous* game, and there always is a *next* game, but the previous game is not temporally earlier than or before the current game, nor is the next game temporally later than or after the current game. There are no temporal relations between games. The moves that happen when the board is being set up again do not happen in the space of chess, since no move of a piece from off the board to its position on the board is a move within the chess board. From every perspective within the game of chess, the appearance of the initial configuration looks like a miracle, like a creative act of God. But that doesn't mean it is one.

There is nothing spatially or temporally outside the universe, since it contains all physical space-time. But there might be something metaphysically beyond or independent of the physical universe. It might be some sort of immaterial spirit world, such as the Platonic World of Forms, or the Christian Heaven and Hell. Nietzsche denies that there is any formal or spiritual world. If there is anything beyond the physical universe, it is the physical universe *again*.

8. The Unit of Recurrence is the Whole Universe

The worst thing that every happened to the idea of recurrence was that it became misunderstood as a *physical* theory. But philosophical theories of eternal recurrence are not physical theories. Today one popular version of the history of the universe says that it started in a "Big Bang", an immense explosion of energy. The Second Law of Thermodynamics says that the universe is gradually "winding down" like a clock: it will die a "heat death" as energy disperses and the universe cools off. According to this theory, the universe keeps expanding forever. If the universe is like that, there is no *physical* recurrence. But that does not mean that there is no recurrence at all.

Every identification of the philosophical theory of the eternal return with any physical theory fails to understand that it simply is not a physical theory. Suppose the universe starts with a Big Bang and then cools down forever into the future. The history of the universe is an infinite series of physical events. But there is nothing impossible (that is, contradictory) about the recurrence of an infinite series of events.

Let the Big Bang occur at time 0; let the next physical event occur at time $1/2$, the next event at time $3/4$, the next event at $7/8$, the next event at $15/16$, and so on. The n-th element in this series has the form $(2^n - 1) / 2^n$, where n is an integer. There are infinitely many integers, so there can be an infinite series of events after the Big Bang at time 0. The series whose events occur at times $(2^n - 1) / 2^n$ is a series whose events get closer and closer to 1 but never reach 1. The series that starts with a Big Bang at time 0 does not define what happens at time 1. Anything could happen. At time 1, there can be *another* Big Bang; the universe it starts then cools down toward its temporal limit at time 2. At time 2, there is another Big Bang; that universe cools down towards its limit at 3. At time n, there is the n-th Big Bang; that universe cools down to its limit at time n+1. Since every series of events that starts with a Big Bang at time n never reaches time n+1, no event at time n+1 has any event that happens before it. The event before $3/4$ is the event at $1/2$, but the event at time 1 has no preceding event. So, none of the Big Bangs at any moment has any cause in the preceding series. The events in each series are entirely physically independent of those before and after. There is no physical connection between the series. Every one of those Big Bangs could begin a physical process that is exactly identical to the one before it.

9. Spatial and Temporal Recurrence

Recurrence of time is not the only kind of recurrence. There are also spatial versions of recurrence, in which the total spatial structure of the universe recurs within the universe. You can combine spatial and temporal recurrence to get spatio-temporal recurrence.

Josiah Royce, an American thinker who lived about the same time as Nietzsche, described a *perfect* map of England that is in England. In this case, the map is a part of the territory and so the map contains an exact copy of itself, but the copy contains an exact copy of itself, and so on, to infinity. It's infinitely self-nested maps:

> A map of England, contained within England, is to represent, down to the minutest detail, every contour and marking, natural or artificial, that occurs upon the surface of England. . . . the map, in order to be complete, according to the rule given, will have to contain, as a part of itself, a representation of its own contour and contents. In order that this representation should be constructed, the representation itself will have to contain once more, as a part of itself, a representation of its own contour and contents; and this representation, in order to be exact, will have once more to contain an image of itself; and so on without limit. . . . We should at once observe that in this one assertion, "A part of England perfectly maps all England, on a smaller scale," there would be implied the assertion not now of a process of trying to draw maps, but of the contemporaneous presence, in England, of an infinite number of maps, of the type just described.[4]

Of course, if something like Royce's map exists, then Royce's own description of it is only half-right. The other half of the story is that what appears to be the England that contains the maps of itself is in fact only a map inside a larger England, which is itself a map within a still larger England. Just as each map contains another map inside it, so also every map is contained by a map that surrounds it.

It's easy to modify Royce's self-nested map to include time. Maps are static. But a movie is like a temporal series of maps: each frame of the movie is a map of one instant of time, it's a map of momentary slice of the universe. So, instead of just a map, suppose there is a perfect movie of England within England. Each frame of the movie contains an exact photographic image of itself within itself on a smaller scale, so that image of the frame contains a perfect image of itself within itself on a still smaller scale. And of course, every frame is contained in a still larger frame. The movie contains the movie, which contains the movie, and so on. If the movie is a repeated series of frames, then the recurrence is both spatial and temporal. Royce's map is 2-dimensional; add a third dimension and you have an endlessly self-nested series of solid 3D maps. Add a 4th dimension for time and you have an endlessly self-nested series of space-time maps -- the physical universe.

10. Trees within Trees

Flip a coin. The event of flipping the coin has two possible outcomes: either heads or tails. To visualize the possibilities, think of two roads diverging. One road is named "Heads" and the other "Tails". You can think of flipping the coin as deciding which of these roads you take. Or you can think of it as simply defining two alternative histories of the coin itself, one in which it lands heads and the other tails. They are both equally real as *possibilities* of the coin.

After you flip the coin once, you can flip it again. So, at the end of each road there is another split. At the end of the "Heads" road there is another "Heads" / "Tails" fork or branch. At the end of the "Tails" road there is another "Heads" / "Tails" fork or branch. The branching network of roads is like a tree. There are four paths in the tree: HH, HT, TH, TT. Each path is a possible history of the coin flipped twice. If you add a "Heads" / "Tails" fork at the end of each of the 4 paths, you have a tree with 8 paths: HHH, HHT, HTH, HTT, THH, THT, TTH, TTT. You can then add a fork at the end of each of the 8 paths, and so on forever. The result is a tree with infinitely many "Heads" / "Tails" branchings. The result is an infinite tree.

Just as you can add another "Heads" / "Tails" branch at the end of any series of branchings, so also you can add one at the start. You can always assume that the coin has been flipped before now, so that the tree of branching possibilities has no beginning. The tree is infinite into the past and into the future.

Every possible series of heads and tails, whether finite or infinite, is in the tree of branching possibilities. All possible histories of the coin are in the tree of branching possibilities. If you only have one coin (an eternal coin), and you flip it over and over again infinitely often, then your flipping of the coin chooses one particular path in the tree. Each time you come to a fork in the road, flip the coin and go down that path till you come to the next fork.

But why restrict yourself to one coin? Or to just one self? At each fork in the road, you and your coin split into divergent copies. You clone yourself and your coin. Now you and your coin are twins, but one of you has a coin with "Heads" up and the other of you has a coin with "Tails" up. The "Heads" up twin goes down the "Heads" branch; the "Tails" up twin goes down the "Tails" branch. At each fork, you divide again. There are infinitely many coins and infinitely many of you. Every possible history of the coin is real.

The infinitely branching tree of possibilities, along with a coin that divides into twins that realize both of its possibilities at each branch, illustrates the combinatorial structure of the will to power. The will to power realizes all possible physical combinations of events, that is, all possible physical histories of the universe. Of course, the point of the example is not that an army of self-dividing twins walks through this structure, all flipping their self-dividing coins as they go. Rather, the point is that every complete series of finite alternatives has the structure of a branching tree of possibilities. The structure is logical: it does not depend on any special physical facts. It depends only on combinatorial facts. The tree is purely mathematical.

Instead of a coin, you could have a 6-sided die. The tree branches 6 ways after every dice toss. Or you can think of each branch in the tree as a possible move in a game. Start with an empty tic-tac-toe grid. Each branch is a move that takes you to a new state of the tic-tac-toe grid, one with another square marked. There are always as many branches as there are possible moves. Once all the squares are marked, the only possibility is to start over with an empty grid. Or start with a chess board in the initial configuration. Each branch is a move that changes the arrangement of pieces on the board. Again, there are as many branches as possible (legal) moves. Once there is checkmate or stalemate, the only possibility is to start over again, to play another game. At the end of every game, there is a tree whose branchings are all possible games. Before the start of every game, there is a tree whose branchings are all possible games.

Any infinite tree of branching possibilities is a self-nested structure just like Royce's perfect map of England within England. Start, for instance, with a chess board in the initial configuration. That board is the root of a chess-tree whose branches are all possible games of chess. At the end of each game-branch, the checkmate or stalemate board is followed by a chess board in the initial configuration, so at the end of every game-branch the whole chess-tree is repeated. If you pick any point in such an infinite tree of possibilities, you will find that it is the root of a tree that contains a subtree with exactly the same branching structure, and that it is itself a subtree in a tree with exactly the same branching structure. It's trees within trees, just like Royce's perfect map of England within England.

If the world as will to power is such an infinitely self-nested tree, then the world contains an exact copy of itself, and is contained by an exact copy of itself. Consequently, every possible series of events occurs infinitely often. Every sequential path in the infinitely self-nested tree is a possible history of the world that contains infinitely many repetitions of every series of events in that history, since the path is infinitely long both into the past and future, and since there are only finitely many alternatives at every branching. Every sequential path in the world is a universe. It is possible to mathematically extend the combinatorial structure of such trees to include infinitely many alternatives at each branching. Any physical theory can exist within such a tree of branching possibilities.

If the world as will to power is an infinitely self-nested tree, then there is eternal recurrence of every history and also of all possible histories. Every finite (and even infinite) history repeats itself. But that is not Nietzsche's deepest point. His deepest point, the deepest of all the lessons to be drawn from the world as will to power, is that *beyond the world there is only the world itself again.* The tree of the world is contained within the tree of the world and contains the tree of the world. This world contains all possible universes. There is no world beyond this world. There is no other world.

11. Past and Future Selves

If the Nietzschean theory of eternal recurrence is right, then there are infinitely many past and future people whose lives and bodies are very similar to your own. Some of them have lives and bodies that are physically identical to your own. There is little doubt that those people are identical to you. There are no physical differences, no biological differences, and (since Nietzsche argues that the mind is a function of the body), no psychological differences. You have many exact duplicates of yourself in the world as will to power. It is hard to deny that you and your exact duplicates are not the same person. In the world as will to power, each person has many instances.

Besides your replicas, there are many people whose bodies and lives are not exactly like yours, but only very similar. You have infinitely many identical twins, where the identity is only genetic. They have the same type of body that you do, because their DNA is the same. Some of these identical twins share much of your history. You and all your identical twins are born of the same parents. But after that, your biographies, characters, and personalities diverge. Still, there is a deep sense in which you and all your identical twins are instances of the person. After all, your life could have been different.

If every possible history of the universe is realized in the world as will to power, then every one of your possible biographies is realized by one of your twins, every possible life is lived. If this is true, it is a powerful antidote to regret and resentment. What do you have to regret? Is there something you wish you had done or not done? One of your twins is doing or not doing it. All your lives are lived.

If your twins know about recurrence of all possible world-histories, then they take the same attitude towards your particular body and biography in this history of the world. You are their twin just as much as they are your twins. This diminishes the intensity of the egotistical attachments that can lead us to condemn this world (GS 162). If you are insulted or injured, if you suffer, then you ought to consider that pain as just a part of the experiences of your *greater self*, which includes all your recurrence twins. Relative to all the pleasure and pain that you are able to experience, every particular pleasure or pain is trivial, all actions are equally great and small (GS 233).

The eternal return leads to an attitude of Stoic detachment. It has an ethical effect. The self is in balance in the world, so our emotions ought to be in balance too. The emotional balance is what the Stoics called *equanimity*. It could also be called *compassion*.

12. Conclusion

My father used to recite this poem: Once in Persia reigned a king, who upon his signet ring, had words of wisdom, these were they: "Even this shall pass away." Nietzsche knows the story:

A certain emperor always bore in mind the transitoriness of all things so as not to take them too seriously and to live at peace among them. To me, on the contrary, everything seems far too valuable to be so fleeting: I seek an eternity for everything: ought one to pour the most precious salves and wines into the sea? -- My consolation is that everything that has been is eternal: the sea will cast it up again. (WP 1065)

Endnotes.

1. Nietzsche says the eternal return "is not only the highest insight, it is also the *profoundest*, the insight most strictly confirmed and maintained by truth and knowledge" (EH 5:2).
2. Eudemus, Frag. 272 in G. S. Kirk & J. E. Raven, *The Presocratic Philosophers* (New York: Cambridge University Press, 1957).
3. D. Hume, *Dialogues Concerning Natural Religion,* part 8.
4. J. Royce, *The World and the Individual* (Supplementary Essay). (New York: Dover, 1959), pp. 504-507. Original work 1899.